RICHARD EBERHART was born in Austin, Minnesota, on April 5, 1904. He was educated at Dartmouth College, Cambridge University, and Harvard. Dartmouth conferred on him its Honorary Doctor of Letters in 1954.

He was tutor to the son of King Prajadhipok of Siam for a year before teaching at St. Mark's School. During World War II he was a naval aircraft gunnery instructor, serving from 1942 to 1946 and becoming a Lieutenant Commander. After the war he was in business in Boston for six years but was called back to teaching in 1952. He was professor or poet in residence at the University of Washington, the University of Connecticut, Wheaton College (Norton, Mass.), and Princeton, and in 1956 was appointed Professor of English and Poet in Residence at Dartmouth.

Oxford University Press in New York and Chatto and Windus in London have published Mr. Eberhart's books concurrently for over a quarter of a century, from his first, *A Bravery of Earth* (1930), to his latest, *The Quarry* (1964). Recent works are *Great Praises* (1957), *Collected Poems 1930–1960* (1960), *Collected Verse Plays* (1962), and the present volume, winner of the Pulitzer Prize for Poetry in 1966.

His other prizes include the Harriet Monroe Memorial Prize, the Harriet Monroe Memorial Award (University of Chicago), the Shelley Memorial Prize, and a grant from the National Institute of Arts and Letters. He was co-winner of the Bollingen Prize from Yale in 1962. Mr. Eberhart was a founder and first president of the Poets' Theatre, Inc., Cambridge, Mass., in 1950.

After serving as Consultant in Poetry at the Library of Congress from 1959 to 1961, he was appointed Honorary Consultant in American Letters, 1963–1966, by the Library of Congress in 1963. He is a member of the Advisory Committee of the John F. Kennedy Center, formerly the National Cultural Center. He gave the Elliston Lectures at the University of Cincinnati in 1961. He is a member of the National Institute of Arts and Letters.

Mr. Eberhart is married and the father of two children.

Richard Eberhart

Selected Poems

1930–1965

New Directions

Acknowledgment is made to Oxford University Press and Chatto and Windus Ltd. for permission to reprint in this volume poems from *Collected Poems 1930–1960*, *The Quarry*, and *Undercliff*. "The Killer" was previously published in *Of Poetry and Power* and *New York Review of Books*, and acknowledgment is made to Basic Books and New York Review of Books for permission to reprint. "The Rush" appeared in the *Proceedings of the National Poetry Festival* (1962), published by the Library of Congress. "Action and Poetry," "At McSorley's Bar," and "The Illusion of Eternity" were published originally in *East Side Review*. "Off Pemaquid" was first printed in the (London) *Times Literary Supplement*. "A Ship Burning and a Comet All in One Day," "The Oak," "Moment of Equilibrium Among the Islands," "Sea Burial from the Cruiser *Reve*," and "The Matin Pandemoniums" appeared originally in *The New Yorker*. "The Face, the Axe and Time" was published earlier in *The Hollins Critic*. A part of the preface is from *Thirty Dartmouth Poems*.

New Directions books are published for James Laughlin
by New Directions Publishing Corporation,
333 Sixth Avenue, New York 14.

Second Printing

Foreword

POETRY is like the mystery of the world. It comes from secret wells; it is a fresh draft from heaven, warmed in earth. (It is made of words, but Mallarmé was limited; words are the vestments of its body.) Every time a man dies we realize that it means more than it did before. It speaks for all our sensibilities. It is spiritual and it is sensuous and in its sensuous meshes the spirit is caught as in a thicket; it tries to release the spirit out of the thicket of our flesh and blood, but is happily caught there. Poetry comes and goes, as subtleties play upon the mind; poetry is a filament, it makes for justice. It states our case, it states the case for mankind. Without it we lack something central; with it we are rich, in opulent throes. We understand what it is to live, to suffer, to hope.

*   *   *

If some wound in the soul were healed there would be no need to write poems. Poetry is continuously aggravating perception into expressing life. It evaluates our unique passage through time. The compulsion to create comes from awareness of being. It is ultimately a recognition of man's estate and of his fate, and ultimately poetry is praise.

1965   *Richard Eberhart*

Contents

Contents

Contents

Contents

THIS FEVERS ME

This fevers me, this sun on green,
On grass glowing, this young spring.
The secret hallowing is come,
Regenerate sudden incarnation,
Mystery made visible
In growth, yet subtly veiled in all,
Ununderstandable in grass,
In flowers, and in the human heart,
This lyric mortal loveliness,
The earth breathing, and the sun.
The young lambs sport, none udderless.
Rabbits dash beneath the brush.
Crocuses have come; wind flowers
Tremble against quick April.
Violets put on the night's blue,
Primroses wear the pale dawn,
The gold daffodils have stolen
From the sun. New grass leaps up;
Gorse yellows, starred with day;
The willow is a graceful dancer
Poised; the poplar poises too.
The apple takes the seafoam's light,
And the evergreen tree is densely bright.
April, April, when will he
Be gaunt, be old, who is so young?
This fevers me, this sun on green,
On grass glowing, this young spring.

I

THE BELLS OF A CHINESE TEMPLE

The bells of a Chinese temple sang
A monody in sunned Sabang,
A singing timbreless of tone,
Like water falling on a stone.
And he was glad, glad to be
A sailor resting from the sea
Where Indians and Arabs go,
Most slowly, slow and slow;
Where swart Malayan women walk
Dreamfully along and talk;
Where skirted, bearded, dark-skin Turks
Go hand in hand, and no one works.
China women with bound doll feet
Like marionettes move down the street,
And underneath the arbored trees,
Mild-eyed, squatting in twos or threes,
Chinamen smoke, peaceful and still,
Gazing afar at the palms on the hill,
Pondering Buddha, these Chinamen—
Or counting their hoarded yen.
And there are girls whose smiles are worth
Some subtle Asiatic mirth
Understood and wonderful:
Girls dark, and shy, and beautiful.

He had not known harbor or town
So free from tumult, fret, or frown,
Of all the sunny towns that are
Spun under a southern star
Upon the Oriental South.
Here Love with amorous mellow mouth
Drinks from the chalice of delight
Sun-mulled wine from dawn till night.
Here the ponderer plucks a lute;
The drowsed land is ripe with fruit;

And all man's conquest and man's glory
Is but a story-teller's story,
Incredible and strangely told
Of men far off amazed with gold,
Who bend beneath some heavy plan
To trample down a fellow-man,
Thus harvest wealth, and fame, and power.

This is Sebang; hour on hour
The full day ripens in the sun,
And time has always just begun.
Primeval silence without stir
Holds the earth like gossamer;
For love is slowly blossoming
In quietness too still to sing,
From which all passions green or ripe
Are shadowy blooms of the Immortal Type.

And here he lingers, murmuring
The name of some forgotten king,
Who had a wonder-welling heart:
Richard Ghormley Eberhart.

FOR A LAMB

I saw on the slant hill a putrid lamb,
Propped with daisies. The sleep looked deep,
The face nudged in the green pillow
But the guts were out for crows to eat.

Where's the lamb? whose tender plaint
Said all for the mute breezes.
Say he's in the wind somewhere,
Say, there's a lamb in the daisies.

'IN A HARD INTELLECTUAL LIGHT'

In a hard intellectual light
I will kill all delight,
And I will build a citadel
Too beautiful to tell

O too austere to tell
And far too beautiful to see,
Whose evident distance
I will call the best of me.

And this light of intellect
Will shine on all my desires,
It will my flesh protect
And flare my bold constant fires,

For the hard intellectual light
Will lay the flesh with nails.
And it will keep the world bright
And closed the body's soft jails.

And from this fair edifice
I shall see, as my eyes blaze,
The moral grandeur of man
Animating all his days.

And peace will marry purpose,
And purity married to grace
Will make the human absolute
As sweet as the human face.

Until my hard vision blears,
And Poverty and Death return
In organ music like the years,
Making the spirit leap, and burn

For the hard intellectual light
That kills all delight
And brings the solemn, inward pain
Of truth into the heart again.

THE GROUNDHOG

In June, amid the golden fields,
I saw a groundhog lying dead.
Dead lay he; my senses shook,
And mind outshot our naked frailty.
There lowly in the vigorous summer
His form began its senseless change,
And made my senses waver dim
Seeing nature ferocious in him.
Inspecting close his maggots' might
And seething cauldron of his being,
Half with loathing, half with a strange love,
I poked him with an angry stick.
The fever arose, became a flame
And Vigour circumscribed the skies,
Immense energy in the sun,
And through my frame a sunless trembling.
My stick had done nor good nor harm.
Then stood I silent in the day
Watching the object, as before;
And kept my reverence for knowledge
Trying for control, to be still,
To quell the passion of the blood;
Until I had bent down on my knees
Praying for joy in the sight of decay.
And so I left; and I returned
In Autumn strict of eye, to see
The sap gone out of the groundhog,
But the bony sodden hulk remained.

But the year had lost its meaning,
And in intellectual chains
I lost both love and loathing,
Mured up in the wall of wisdom.
Another summer took the fields again
Massive and burning, full of life,
But when I chanced upon the spot
There was only a little hair left,
And bones bleaching in the sunlight
Beautiful as architecture;
I watched them like a geometer,
And cut a walking stick from a birch.
It has been three years, now.
There is no sign of the groundhog.
I stood there in the whirling summer,
My hand capped a withered heart,
And thought of China and of Greece,
Of Alexander in his tent;
Of Montaigne in his tower,
Of Saint Theresa in her wild lament.

MAZE

I have a tree in my arm,
There are two hounds in my feet,
The earth can do me no harm
And the lake of my eyes is sweet.

But a fire has burnt the tree down,
I have no blood for the hounds.
Why has the will made me a crown
For a human mind that has bounds?

Who made the tree? Who made fire?
The hounds have gone back to the master.
The earth has killed my desire
That leaped up faster and faster.

It is man did it, man,
Who imagined imagination,
And he did what man can,
He uncreated creation.

There is no tree in my arm,
I have no hounds in my feet,
The earth can soothe me and harm,
And the lake of my eyes is a cheat.

'WHERE ARE THOSE HIGH AND HAUNTING SKIES'

Where are those high and haunting skies,
Higher than the see-through wind? Where are
The rocky springs beyond desire? And where
The sudden source of purity?

Now they are gone again. Though world
Decrease the wraith-like eye so holy,
And bring a summer in, and with it folly,
Though the senses bless and quell,

I would not with such blessings be beguiled.
But seek an image far more dear. Oh where
Has gone that madness wild? Where stays
The abrupt essence and the final shield?

1934

Caught upon a thousand thorns, I sing,
Like a rag in the wind,
Caught in the blares of the automobile horns
And on the falling airplane's wing.
Caught napping in my study
Among a thousand books of poetry.

Doing the same thing over and over again
Brings about an obliteration of pain.
Each day dies in a paper litter
As the heart becomes less like a rapier.
In complexity, feeling myself absurd
Dictating an arbitrary word,

My self my own worst enemy,
Hunting the past through all its fears,
That on the brain that glory burst
Bombing a ragged future's story,
Caught in iron individuality
As in the backwash of a sea

Knowing not whether to fight out,
Or keep silent; to talk about the weather,
Or rage again through wrong and right,
Knowing knowledge is a norm of nothing,
And I have been to the Eastern seas
And walked on all the Hebrides.

Ashamed of loving a long-practised selfhood,
Lost in a luxury of speculation,
At the straight grain of a pipe I stare
And spit upon all worlds of Spain;
Time like a certain sedative
Quelling the growth of the purpose tree.

Aware of the futility of action,
Of the futility of prayer aware,
Trying to pry from the vest of poetry
The golden heart of mankind's deep despair,
Unworthy of a simple love
In august, elected worlds to move

Stern, pliant in the modern world, I sing,
Afraid of nothing and afraid of everything,
Curtailing joy, withholding irony,

Pleased to condemn contemporaneity
Seeking the reality, skirting
The dangerous absolutes of fear and hope,

And I have eased reality and fiction
Into a kind of intellectual fruition
Strength in solitude, life in death,
Compassion by suffering, love in strife,
And ever and still the weight of mystery
Arrows a way between my words and me.

'WHEN DORIS DANCED'

When Doris danced under the oak tree
The sun himself might wish to see,
Might bend beneath those lovers, leaves,
While her her virgin step she weaves
And envious cast his famous hue
To make her daft, yet win her too.

When Doris danced under the oak tree
Slow John, so stormed in heart, at sea
Gone all his store, a wreck he lay.
But on the ground the sun-beams play.
They lit his face in such degree
Doris lay down, all out of pity.

EXPERIENCE EVOKED

Now come to me all men
With savagery and innocence,
With axe to chop the fir tree,
Or seed, small, for the immense
Sewing of earth with old Rose.

9

Now come all men, arrayed
With the colours of the garden
Around them where they stayed
Till bone began to harden
Under the thinning of the nose.
Come all men, unto whom
Wind was a snarling wire whip
In the contusions of a doom
And with red flecks on their lip
They leaped up, danced, grew tall.
Come all, the babe bound
In terror and panic cry;
Or an old man found
With a skylark in his eye.
Come, harsh shroud over all.

TWO LOVES

That her serene influence should spread
An afternoon of soft autumnal light
Is to my heart not unaccountable
For she was young, and is not dead.
And still her cheek is red and white.

But that this stealthy still insistent power
Pervades my mind and will not slumber me
Is delicate woe and glory hard to bear;
Her life lives in a ghost-wrought hour,
From whose chill spirit I am not free.

The one was willow to an ardent touch
And she was mood that had a right to die.
But she, the other, the passion of my mind
Long-living still, does overmuch
Come from the dead, and from the sky.

BURDEN

Whoever lives beside a mountain knows,
Although he dares not speak it out, that he
Must always carry on his heart the snows
That burden down the trees. And never the sea
Will rush around him cool, like snow-cool air,
And carry him and lift him like a leaf.
He will not find this lightness anywhere
Since mountains brood, they hold dark league with grief.

The pine trees never tire of moving down
The slopes to meet him, pointing up from town
Beyond the tree-line to the rigid peaks.
The mountain holds him though it never speaks.
He scrambles over boulders on his knees
Trying to reach the summit, like the trees.

WHAT IF REMEMBRANCE?

When I am lying under
A roof of green grass
That trembles when the thunder
And the white rain pass

And all my meaning gone
In the rhythmic turn of earth,
Senseless under the lawn
Even when grass takes birth

What if remembrance should come
Into the earth of my brain
And all my being plumb
Again
Pain?

'IN PRISONS OF ESTABLISHED CRAZE'

In prisons of established craze
Hear the sane tread without noise
Whose songs no iron walls will raze
Though hearts are as of girls or boys.
By the waters burning clear
Where sheds of men are only seen,
Accept eloquent time, and revere
The silence of the great machine.
On the sweet earth green and moist
When vainglorious cities magnify,
The senseless dissonance will foist
As witless on the shining sky.
There is some stealth in rhythm yet
Albeit an even breath is not.
In the mind is a gauge set,
Lest the blood spill, and blot.

'NOW IS THE AIR MADE OF CHIMING BALLS'

Now is the air made of chiming balls.
The stormcloud, wizened, has rolled its rind away.
Now is the eye with hill and valley laved
And the seeds, assuaged, peep from the nested spray.
The bluebird drops from a bough. The speckled meadow-lark
Springs in his lithe array. Fresh air
Blesses the vanished tear; the bunched anguish.
The laughing balls their joyful pleasure tear.
Renewed is the whole world and the sun
Begins to dress with warmth again every thing.
The lettuce in pale burn; the burdock tightening;
And naked necks of craning fledglings.

'WHEN GOLDEN FLIES UPON MY CARCASS COME'

When golden flies upon my carcass come,
Those pretty monsters, shining globules
Like tautened oily suns, and congregate
Fixing their several gems upon one core
That shines a blossom then of burning gold,
'Tis as the sun's burning glass and diadem
They work, at the first chance of rotten flesh,
And, senseless little messengers of time,
Some beauty keep even at the guts of things,
Which is a fox caught, and I watch the flies.

RECOLLECTION OF CHILDHOOD

O the jungle is beautiful the jungle is wild
Here are the rodents and the butterflies,
The thorn tree prickles and the shady grottoes,
And I'll lie in the sun all day, and the shade.

And here is the orchard, bulging big fruit,
Adazzle in the eyes all red and golden,
There is the barn, and the many cows,
Hurray for the hay, I'll fall and tumble in the hay.

And below the happy pasture green and moist
I'll walk it to the shady grove by the river,
Swim the clear stream, the chalk cliff climb,
Bursting with desire still—cease action never,

But in the natural world of happy forms
Bird, beast, tree, fern, earth and rain and sun
Live melodious love, and touch above
All fingered air the very god of love.

'THE CRITIC WITH HIS PAINED EYE'

The critic with his pained eye
Cannot my source espy
For truly and purely to eye it
He would have as Critic to die.

I with joyful vision see,
I cannot his purpose acquire.
For if the Critic were truly free
He would love, and not be a liar.

ORCHARD

I

Lovely were the fruit trees in the evening.
We sat in the automobile all five of us,
Full of the silence of deep grieving,
For tragedy stalked among the fruit trees.

Strongest was the father, of solid years,
Who set his jaw against the coming winter,
Pure, hard, strong, and infinitely gentle
For the worst that evil brings can only kill us.

Most glorious was the mother, beautiful
Who in the middle course of life was stalked
By the stark shape of malignant disease,
And her face was holy white like all desire.

And we three, in our benumbing youngness,
Half afraid to guess at the danger there,
Looked in stillness at the glowing fruit trees,
While tumultuous passions raged in the air.

II

And the first, the father, with indomitable will
Strove in iron decision, in all human strength
With a powerful complete contempt of defeat,
Six feet of manhood and not a mark of fear.

And the next, the mother, wonderfully mild,
Wise with the wisdom that never changes,
Poured forth her love divinely magnified
We knew not by what imminent despair.

While the older brother and the younger,
Separate, yet placed in the first light
Of brutal recognition, held a trembling sister
Who knew not the trial of fortitude to come.

And in the evening, among the warm fruit trees
All of life and all of death were there,
Of pain unto death, of struggle to endure,
And the strong right of human love was there.

THE HUMANIST

Hunting for the truly human
I looked for the true man
And saw an ape at the fair
With the circle still to square. Learning
Breeds its own ignorance. Fame and power
Demand a rush and pounding.
Those who rush through rush through, and who
Are they but those who rush through?
Yet truth resides in contemplation
And comprehension of contemplation
Not necessarily of Plato. Action explains

A field full of folk and golden football flexions,
Action for actors. Truth through contemplation
Resurrects the truly human,
Makes known the true man
Whom these lines can scan:
But miss his secret final point.
The world is too much in joint. No use
Setting that right, that squaring, that harrying: for
The true man lives in mystery
Of God; God his agile soul will see
But he will not see God's majesty,
And that is what makes you and me
Whether man or woman
Neither true nor free
But truly human.

'I WENT TO SEE IRVING BABBITT'

I went to see Irving Babbitt
In the Eighteenth Century clean and neat
When he opened his mouth to speak French
I fell clean off my seat.

He spoke it not fair and fetisly
But harshly laboured it like a Yankee
Even as my nubian Swahili
Is sweet and pleasant to me.

And when we went out of the critical door
Crying for more, crying for more
I saw the hater of mechanical America
Bulge through the Square in a critical Ford.

Harvard is a good place, Harvard is the best,
Among the immemorial elms you'll come to rest
Strolling the Yard, the only proper yardstick,
Warbling your native foot-notes mild.

'THE GOAL OF INTELLECTUAL MAN'

The goal of intellectual man
Striving to do what he can
To bring down out of uncreated light
Illumination to our night

Is not possession of the fire
Annihilation of his own desire
To the source a secret soaring
And all his self outpouring

Nor is it an imageless place
Wherein there is no human face
Nor laws, nor hierarchies, nor dooms
And only the cold weight of the tomb

But it is human love, love
Concrete, specific, in a natural move
Gathering goodness, it is free
In the blood as in the mind's harmony,

It is love discoverable here
Difficult, dangerous, pure, clear,
The truth of the positive hour
Composing all of human power.

'IMAGINING HOW IT WOULD BE TO BE DEAD'

Imagining how it would be to be dead,
Until my tender filaments
From mere threads air have become
And this is all my consciousness
(While like a world of rock and stone
My body cumbersome and big
Breathes out a vivid atmosphere

Which is the touchless breach of the air)
I lost my head, and could not hold
Either my hands together or my heart
But was so sentient a being
I seemed to break time apart
And thus became all things air can touch
Or could touch could it touch all things,
And this was an embrace most dear,
Final, complete, a flying without wings.
From being bound to one poor skull,
And that surrounded by one earth,
And the earth in one universe forced,
And that chained to some larger gear,
I was the air, I was the air,
And then I pressed on eye and cheek
The sightless hinges of eternity
That make the whole world creak.

'IF I COULD ONLY LIVE AT THE PITCH THAT IS NEAR MADNESS'

If I could only live at the pitch that is near madness
When everything is as it was in my childhood
Violent, vivid, and of infinite possibility:
That the sun and the moon broke over my head.

Then I cast time out of the trees and fields,
Then I stood immaculate in the Ego;
Then I eyed the world with all delight,
Reality was the perfection of my sight.

And time has big handles on the hands,
Fields and trees a way of being themselves.
I saw battalions of the race of mankind
Standing stolid, demanding a moral answer.

I gave the moral answer and I died
And into a realm of complexity came
Where nothing is possible but necessity
And the truth wailing there like a red babe.

'COVER ME OVER'

Cover me over, clover;
Cover me over, grass.
The mellow day is over
And there is night to pass.

Green arms about my head,
Green fingers on my hands.
Earth has no quieter bed
In all her quiet lands.

'I WALKED OVER THE GRAVE
OF HENRY JAMES'

I walked over the grave of Henry James
But recently, and one eye kept the dry stone.
The other leaned on boys at games away,
My soul was balanced in my body cold.

I am one of those prodigals of hell
Whom ten years have seen cram with battle;
Returns to what he canted from, grants it good,
As asthma makes itself a new resolution.

I crushed a knob of earth between my fingers,
This is a very ordinary experience.
A name may be glorious but death is death,
I thought, and took a street-car back to Harvard Square.

RUMINATION

When I can hold a stone within my hand
And feel time make it sand and soil, and see
The roots of living things grow in this land,
Pushing between my fingers flower and tree,
Then I shall be as wise as death,
For death has done this and he will
Do this to me, and blow his breath
To fire my clay, when I am still.

'MYSTICISM HAS NOT THE PATIENCE TO WAIT FOR GOD'S REVELATION'

KIERKEGAARD

But to reach the archimedean point
Was all my steadfastness;
The disjointed times to teach
Courage from what is dreadful.

It was the glimpses in the lightning
Made me a sage, but made me say
No word to make another fight,
My own fighting heart full of dismay.

Spirit, soul, and fire are reached!
And springs of the mind, like springs of the feet
Tell all, all know, nothing wavers there!
All the flowers of the heart turn to ice-flowers,

Heaviness of the world prevailing
('The higher we go the more terrible it is')
Duplicity of man, heart-hate,
The hypocrite, the vain, the whipper, the cheat,

The eternal ape on the leash,
Drawing us down to faith,
Which the Greeks call divine folly,
The tug of laughter and of irony.

'I WALKED OUT TO THE GRAVEYARD
TO SEE THE DEAD'

I walked out to the graveyard to see the dead
The iron gates were locked, I couldn't get in,
A golden pheasant on the dark fir boughs
Looked with fearful method at the sunset,

Said I, Sir bird, wink no more at me
I have had enough of my dark eye-smarting,
I cannot adore you, nor do I praise you,
But assign you to the rafters of Montaigne.

Who talks with the Absolute salutes a Shadow,
Who seeks himself shall lose himself;
And the golden pheasants are no help
And action must be learned from love of man.

THE SOUL LONGS TO RETURN
WHENCE IT CAME

I drove up to the graveyard, which
Used to frighten me as a boy,
When I walked down the river past it,
And evening was coming on. I'd make sure
I came home from the woods early enough.
I drove in, I found to the place, I

Left the motor running. My eyes hurried,
To recognize the great oak tree
On the little slope, among the stones.
It was a high day, a crisp day,
The cleanest kind of Autumn day,
With brisk intoxicating air, a
Little wind that frisked, yet there was
Old age in the atmosphere, nostalgia,
The subtle heaviness of the Fall.
I stilled the motor. I walked a few paces;
It was good, the tree; the friendliness of it.
I touched it, I thought of the roots;
They would have pierced her seven years.
O all peoples! O mighty shadows!
My eyes opened along the avenue
Of tombstones, the common land of death.
Humiliation of all loves lost,
That might have had full meaning in any
Plot of ground, come, hear the silence,
See the quivering light. My mind worked
Almost imperceptibly, I
In the command, I the wilful ponderer.
I must have stood silent and thoughtful
There. A host of dry leaves
Danced on the ground in the wind.
They startled, they curved up from the **ground,**
There was a dry rustling, rattling.
The sun was motionless and brittle.
I felt the blood darken in my cheeks
And burn. Like running. My eyes
Telescoped on decay, I out of command.
Fear, tenderness, they seized me.
My eyes were hot, I dared not look
At the leaves. A pagan urge swept me.
Multitudes, O multitudes in one.
The urge of the earth, the titan
Wild and primitive lust, fused
On the ground of her grave.

I was a being of feeling alone.
I flung myself down on the earth
Full length on the great earth, full length,
I wept out the dark load of human love.
In pagan adoration I adored her.
I felt the actual earth of her.
Victor and victim of humility,
I closed in the wordless ecstasy
Of mystery: where there is no thought
But feeling lost in itself forever,
Profound, remote, immediate, and calm.
Frightened, I stood up, I looked about
Suspiciously, hurriedly (a rustling),
As if the sun, the air, the trees
Were human, might not understand.
I drew breath, it made a sound,
I stepped gingerly away. Then
The mind came like a fire, it
Tortured man, I thought of madness.
The mind will not accept the blood.
The sun and sky, the trees and grasses,
And the whispering leaves, took on
Their usual characters. I went away,
Slowly, tingling, elated, saying, saying
Mother, Great Being, O Source of Life
To whom in wisdom we return,
Accept this humble servant evermore.

RETROSPECTIVE FORELOOK

The logical pleasure of expectant mercy
Will be an end of us, will make an end.
The demon pulling us from the peach orchard
Where we were uninfected, ineffectual in time,
Cannot get off our skins; we did not win,
But entered more fully the manhood of sin.

The book of Boehme, being tired after bicycling,
The visionary voluptuary asleep in the hay,
All that effort in the fresh fields of the French,
These were days were prayers were potent maskers,
Fame on his forehead, the gust a good gear,
Where now the glory of the ghostly year?

Pascal, too, the attic full of strife and charm,
Mozart a checkerwork of lilacs; Descartes,
Who in his statue, strangely singular in Tours,
Set the savage mirror in the delving eye,
These were pilgrims come to country new
To pommel, hearten, sing, seem, and sue.

The old vexation of the moon! Climbing Chartres,
Where on the windy roof, midst gargoyles intricate,
What moonlight and what noonday imaginings
Compelled the reason and made dim the blood
In shadows of the past over the champaign
In silent noonlong or roan night of rain.

While in that vault where mostly man makes God,
The hallowed light at evening dimly falls,
(the dimness of the nave gravely the light recalls)
But falling brings the glow and golden growth
Of vague, supernatural, spiritual pressures
where the weight of our redemption seems
A compilation of and nurse of dreams.

And long were days and tall were tremble-trees,
The symbol of the self lost in a haze.
And errors of sentience, O senses sweet! sour! sweet!
That ravelled out your substance quizzically,
To go forward and to retreat, to gain
And lose, and never to quite see the truth plain!

That struggle of all Europe! The massive English means
Contiguous to reason, lapsed in jiggly greens,
Where heart was pierced, harrowed the head, was bride

To lust of learning, and the whole eye acquist.
There were the centuries a valid looks,
On English faces no need to read the books.

The demon drives us and we have to go.
The dangerous mountains never climbed aspired to,
While tops of standing, dancing places, are descried.
Consciousness it is that blights us all,
Visionary candor in the branches
Hallucinatory avalanche the pandar.

While stealing through the nave so ancient seeming
The truth of metaphysical reason there concordant,
Stark Lenin, radiant, with blood upon his head
And hands like hams that fed a famished land
Was all that subtlety is worth, and more,
Was the West, was what the world would be.

NEW HAMPSHIRE, FEBRUARY

Nature had made them hide in crevices,
Two wasps so cold they looked like bark.
Why I do not know, but I took them
And I put them
In a metal pan, both day and dark.

Like God touching his finger to Adam
I felt, and thought of Michaelangelo,
For whenever I breathed on them,
The slightest breath,
They leaped, and preened as if to go.

My breath controlled them always quite.
More sensitive than electric sparks
They came into life
Or they withdrew to ice,
While I watched, suspending remarks.

Then one in a blind career got out,
And fell to the kitchen floor. I
Crushed him with my cold ski boot,
By accident. The other
Had not the wit to try or die.

And so the other is still my pet.
The moral of this is plain.
But I will shirk it.
You will not like it. And
God does not live to explain.

THE HORSE CHESTNUT TREE

Boys in sporadic but tenacious droves
Come with sticks, as certainly as Autumn,
To assault the great horse chestnut tree.

There is a law governs their lawlessness.
Desire is in them for a shining amulet
And the best are those that are highest up.

They will not pick them easily from the ground.
With shrill arms they fling to the higher branches,
To hurry the work of nature for their pleasure.

I have seen them trooping down the street
Their pockets stuffed with chestnuts shucked, unshucked.
It is only evening keeps them from their wish.

Sometimes I run out in a kind of rage
To chase the boys away: I catch an arm,
Maybe, and laugh to think of being the lawgiver.

I was once such a young sprout myself
And fingered in my pocket the prize and trophy.
But still I moralize upon the day

And see that we, outlaws on God's property,
Fling out imagination beyond the skies,
Wishing a tangible good from the unknown.

And likewise death will drive us from the scene
With the great flowering world unbroken yet,
Which we held in idea, a little handful.

'GO TO THE SHINE THAT'S ON A TREE'

Go to the shine that's on a tree
When dawn has laved with liquid light
With luminous light the nighted tree
And take that glory without fright.

Go to the song that's in a bird
When he has seen the glistening tree,
That glorious tree the bird has heard
Give praise for its felicity.

Then go to the earth and touch it keen,
Be tree and bird, be wide aware
Be wild aware of light unseen,
And unheard song along the air.

AT NIGHT

In the dust are my father's beautiful hands,
In the dust are my mother's eyes.
Here by the shore of the ocean standing,
Watching: still I do not understand.

Love flows over me, around me,
Here at night by the sea, by the sovereign sea.

Gone is that bone-hoard of strength;
Gone her gentle motion laughing, walking.

Is it not strange that disease and death
Should rest, by the undulant sea?

And I stare, rich with gifts, alone,

Feeling from the sea those terrene presences,
My father's hands, my mother's eyes.

DAM NECK, VIRGINIA

Anti-aircraft seen from a certain distance
On a steely blue night say a mile away
Flowers on the air absolutely dream-like,
The vision has no relation to the reality.

The floating balls of light are tossed easily
And float out into space without a care,
They the sailors of the gentlest parabolas
In a companionship and with a kind of stare.

They are a controlled kind of falling stars,
But not falling, rising and floating and going out,
Teaming together in efflorescent spectacle
Seemingly better than nature's: man is on the lookout.

The men are firing tracers, practising at night.
Each specialist himself precision's instrument,
These expert prestidigitators press the luminence
In knowledge of and ignorance of their doing.

They do not know the dream-like vision ascending
In me, one mile away: they had not thought of that.
Huddled in darkness behind their bright projectors
They are the scientists of the skill to kill.

28

As this sight and show is gentle and false,
The truth of guns is fierce that aims at death.
Of war in the animal sinews let us speak not,
But of the beautiful disrelation of the spiritual.

THE FURY OF AERIAL BOMBARDMENT

You would think the fury of aerial bombardment
Would rouse God to relent; the infinite spaces
Are still silent. He looks on shock-pried faces.
History, even, does not know what is meant.

You would feel that after so many centuries
God would give man to repent; yet he can kill
As Cain could, but with multitudinous will,
No farther advanced than in his ancient furies.

Was man made stupid to see his own stupidity?
Is God by definition indifferent, beyond us all?
Is the eternal truth man's fighting soul
Wherein the Beast ravens in its own avidity?

Of Van Wettering I speak, and Averill,
Names on a list, whose faces I do not recall
But they are gone to early death, who late in school
Distinguished the belt feed lever from the belt holding pawl.

WORLD WAR

Flutesong willow winding weather,
Tomorrow lovely undulant today,
Glorious bird glide in forest glade,
In meadow golden lissom girl dance,

Tremble air with never yesterday,
Grassy twirling boyfoot triumphing,

Budding bough drops lovely lording,
Pearling cuckoobrook cool ecstasy,

Woven from lucid sunny nest,
World of mellow willow mist,
Now forever pleasures piping,
Honey supple body wonderful:

Strike down, batter! shatter! splinter!
Destroy! fracture! cripple! butcher!
Knock! beat! whack! cuff !
Ruin! gash! smash! blast!

Baby Red Breasted Chained Nippled,
Pavement Clattering People Crippled,
Youth Courageous Finger Felled,
Nutty Manhood Maggot Shelled,

Buzzards Smiling Char the Sky,
Pain Caressing Bites the Eye,
Grass Has Adders Time Vipers,
The Heart Burns its Lifted Ladders,

Howls the Whirlwind Over the World,
Tempests Quaking Shake the World,
The Earthquake Opens Abrupt the World,
Cold Dreadful Mass Destruction.

THE CANCER CELLS

Today I saw a picture of the cancer cells,
Sinister shapes with menacing attitudes.
They had outgrown their test-tube and advanced,
Sinister shapes with menacing attitudes,
Into a world beyond, a virulent laughing gang.
They looked like art itself, like the artist's mind,

Powerful shaker, and the taker of new forms.
Some are revulsed to see these spiky shapes;
It is the world of the future too come to.
Nothing could be more vivid than their language,
Lethal, sparkling and irregular stars,
The murderous design of the universe,
The hectic dance of the passionate cancer cells.
O just phenomena to the calculating eye,
Originals of imagination. I flew
With them in a piled exuberance of time,
My own malignance in their racy, beautiful gestures
Quick and lean: and in their riot too
I saw the stance of the artist's make,
The fixed form in the massive fluxion.

I think Leonardo would have in his disinterest
Enjoyed them precisely with a sharp pencil.

INDIAN PIPE

Searching once I found a flower
    By a sluggish stream.
Waxy white, a stealthy tower
    To an Indian's dream.
    This its life supreme.

Blood red winds the sallow creek
    Draining as it flows.
Left the flower all white and sleek,
    Fainting in repose.
    Gentler than a rose.

Red man's pipe is now a ghost
    Whispering to beware.
Hinting of the savage host
    Once that travelled there.
    Perfume frail as air.

FORMS OF THE HUMAN

I wanted to be more human
For I felt I thought too much
And for all the thinking I did—
More rabbits in the same hutch.

And how to be more human, I said?
I will tell you the way, I said.
I know how to do it, I said.
But what I said was not what I did.

I took an old garden hoe
And dug the earth, and planted there,
Not forgetting the compost too,
Three small beans that one might grow.

Three grew tall, but one was wild
So I cut off the other two,
And now I have a wild bean flower
The sweetest that ever grew.

SEALS, TERNS, TIME

The seals at play off Western Isle
In the loose flowing of the summer tide
And burden of our strange estate—

Resting on the oar and lolling on the sea,
I saw their curious images,
Hypnotic, sympathetic eyes

As the deep elapses of the soul.
O ancient blood, O blurred kind forms
That rise and peer from elemental water:

I loll upon the oar, I think upon the day,
Drawn by strong, by the animal soft bonds
Back to a dim pre-history;

While off the point of Jagged Light
In hundreds, gracefully, the fork-tailed terns
Draw swift esprits across the sky.

Their aspirations dip in mine,
The quick order of their changing spirit,
More freedom than the eye can see.

Resting lightly on the oarlocks,
Pondering, and balanced on the sea,
A gauze and spindrift of the world,

I am in compulsion hid and thwarted,
Pulled back in the mammal water,
Enticed to the release of the sky.

A LEGEND OF VIABLE WOMEN

I

Maia was one, all gold, fire, and sapphire,
Bedazzling of intelligence that rinsed the senses,
She was of Roman vocables the disburser,
Six courtiers in Paris sat to her hats.

There was Anna, the cool Western evidencer
Who far afield sought surrender in Sicily,
Wept under the rose window of Palma de Mallorca,
For she thought fate had played a child in her hand.

There was Betty the vigorous; her Packard of Philadelphia
Spurred she; she was at home in Tanganyika,
Who delighted to kill the wild elephant,
Went Eastward on, to the black tigers of Indochine.

There was Margaret of Germany in America, and Jerusalem,
Of mild big eyes, who loved the blood of Englishmen,
Safely to voyage the Eros battlements of Europe,
Protectress to be of young and home, massive the mother.

There was Helen the blond Iowan, actress raddled,
Who dared learning a little, of coyness the teacher,
Laughing subtleties, manipulator of men, a Waldorf
Of elegant fluff, endangering to the serious.

There was Jeannette the cool and long, bright of tooth,
Lady of gay friendship, and of authentic song,
Beyond and indifferent to the male seduction
Who to art pledged all her nature's want and call.

There was the sultry Emma of West Virginia,
Calf-eyed, velvet of flesh, mature in youngness,
Gentle the eager learner of nature's dimensions,
Always to her controlling womanhood in thrall.

There was Sue, the quick, the artful, the dashing,
Who broke all the laws; a Villager in her own apartment,
She was baffled by the brains of Plato and Aristotle,
Whose mind contained most modern conceptions.

There was Maxine, a woman of fire and malice
Who knew of revenge and subterfuge the skills,
A dominator, a thin beauty, a woman of arts and letters;
She of many psychological infidelities.

There was savage Catherine, who leaped into the underground,
Her female anger thrown at abstract injustice.
And she could match her wits with international man,
A glory, a wreaker, alas, who now posthumous is.

There was Madge the sinister, who raged through husbands
    three.
She was somdel Groddeckian, a spendthrift of morality;
Existentialist that with men was dexterous
And would be in ten years after thirty, thirty-three.

There was a nun of modesty, who with service was heavy
And big with sweet acts all her sweet life long;
Enough wisdom she had for twenty ordinary women
Who percepted love as a breath, and as a song.

II

Where is Kimiko, the alabaster girl of Tokyo,
Living in bamboo among rustling scents and innuendoes,
To whom from Hatteras, the Horn, or Terra del Fuego
Returned as to a starry placement the sea voyager?

Where has time cyclic eventuated Vera
The proud noblewoman of Vienna? Among opera lights
She lived in a gaiety of possessive disasters,
Abandoned to the retaliatory shores of music.

Where is the naked brown girl of the nipa hut,
Under fronds, to Mount Mayon's perfect symmetry,
From the wash of the sea, looking from Legaspi?
Where in nature is this form, so brown, so fair, so free?

Where, who, sold into slavery in white Shanghai,
Walked and breathed in grace on Bubbling Well Road,
Subject to ancient sinuosities and patience,
Whose power was to represent unquestioning obedience?

Where is Hortense, the hermetically sealed?
Where is Hermione, haunted by heavens, who hesitated?
Where is Lucy, of bees and liberty the lover?
Where is Eustacia, of marionettes and Austrian dolls?

III

There were prideful women; women of blood and lust;
Patient women who rouged with scholarship's dust;
There were women who touched the soul of the piano;
Women as cat to mouse with their psychoanalyst.

There were women who did not understand themselves
Locking and unlocking misery's largess yearly;
Fabulous women who could not manumit the world
And babbled in syllables of the past and of money.

There were women committed to sins of treachery
The aborters of privilege and of nature's necessity;
There were the sinners in acedia of frigidity
Who negated even the grossness and grandeur of fear.

There were women without tenderness or pity
There were those more male than feminine men
Who rode the horses of their strident fury,
To whom subtle time made a passing bow.

There were independent women of society
Whose proud wisdom was their father's will.
There were mysterious women, Egyptian as a scarab
To whom scent and sound were a mysterious recall.

IV

Women are like the sea, and wash upon the world
In unalterable tides under the yellowing moon
Whose essential spirit is like nature's own,
To man the shadowy waters, the great room.

They come and go in tides of passion, and show
The melancholy at the heart of fullness,
Time crumples them, these vessels of the generations
Are crushed on the rocks as the green sea urchins.

They are the flesh in its rich, watery symbol,
A summer in July under the tenderest moon,
An island in the sea invincible to touch,
A refuge in man against refulgent ideation.

Women have gone where roll the sea bells
In the long, slow, the wide and the clear waters;
Their flesh which is our love and our loss
Has become the waste waters of the ocean swell.

They are the mothers of man's intelligence
To whom he is held by umbilical time,
And far though he roam, to treat with imagination,
He is brought home to her, as she brings a child.

A SHIP BURNING
AND A COMET ALL IN ONE DAY

When the tide was out
And the sea was quiet,
We hauled the boat to the edge,
On a fair day in August,
As who, all believing,
Would give decent burial
To the life of a used boat,
Not leave a corpse above ground.

And some, setting fires
On the old and broken deck,
Poured on the kerosene
With a stately quietude,
Measuring out departure,
And others brought libations
In red glasses to the sea's edge,
And all held one in hand.

Then the Captain arose
And poured spirit over the prow
And the sparks flew upward
And consigned her with fierce
Cry and fervent prayer
To immortal transubstantiation.
And the pure nature of air
Received her grace and charm.

And evening came on the sea
As the whole company
Sat upon the harsh rocks
Watching the tide come in
And take the last debris,
And when it became dark
A great comet appeared in the sky
With a star in its nether tail.

GREAT PRAISES

Great praises of the summer come
With the flushed hot air
Burdening the branches.

Great praises are in the air!
For such a heat as this
We have sweated out our lives toward death.

I used to hate the summer ardour
In all my intellectual pride,
But now I love the very order

That brushed me fast aside,
And rides upon the air of the world
With insolent, supernal splendour.

THE TOBACCONIST OF EIGHTH STREET

I saw a querulous old man, the tobacconist of Eighth Street.
Scales he had, and he would mix tobacco with his hands
And pour the fragrance in a paper bag.
You walked out selfishly upon the city.

Some ten years I watched him. Fields of Eire
Or of Arabia were in his voice. He strove to please.
The weights of age, of fear were in his eyes,
And on his neck time's cutting edge.

One year I crossed his door. Time had crossed before.
Collapse had come upon him, the collapse of affairs.
He was sick with revolution,
Crepitant with revelation.

And I went howling into the crooked streets,
Smashed with recognition: for him I flayed the air,
For him cried out, and sent a useless prayer
To the disjointed stones that were his only name:

Such insight is one's own death rattling past.

ON SHOOTING PARTICLES BEYOND
THE WORLD

"*White Sands, N.M. Dec.* 18 (*UP*). '*We first throw a little something into the skies,*' *Zwicky said.* '*Then a little more, then a shipload of instruments—then ourselves*'."

On this day man's disgust is known
Incipient before but now full blown
With minor wars of major consequence,
Duly building empirical delusions.

Now this little creature in a rage
Like new-born infant screaming compleat angler
Objects to the whole globe itself
And with a vicious lunge he throws

Metal particles beyond the orbit of mankind.
Beethoven shaking his fist at death,
A giant dignity in human terms,
Is nothing to this imbecile metal fury.

The world is too much for him. The green
Of earth is not enough, love's deities,
Peaceful intercourse, happiness of nations,
The wild animal dazzled on the desert.

If the maniac would only realize
The comforts of his padded cell
He would have penetrated the
Impenetrability of the spiritual.

It is not intelligent to go too far.
How he frets that he can't go too!
But his particles would maim a star,
His free-floating bombards rock the moon.

Good Boy! We pat the baby to eructate,
We pat him then for eructation.
Good Boy Man! Your innards are put out,
From now all space will be your vomitorium.

The atom bomb accepted this world,
Its hatred of man blew death in his face.
But not content, he'll send slugs beyond,
His particles of intellect will spit on the sun.

Not God he'll catch, in the mystery of space.
He flaunts his own out-cast state
As he throws his imperfections outward bound,
And his shout that gives a hissing sound.

THE HUMAN BEING IS A
LONELY CREATURE

It is borne in upon me that pain
Is essential. The bones refuse to act.
Recalcitrancy is life's fine flower.
The human being is a lonely creature.

Fear is of the essence. You do not fear?
I say you lie. Fear is the truth of time.
If it is not now, it will come hereafter.
Death is waiting for the human creature.

Praise to harmony and love.
They are best, all else is false.
Yet even in love and harmony
The human being is a lonely creature.

The old sloughed off, the new new-born,
What fate and what high hazards join
As life tries out the soul's enterprise.
Time is waiting for the human creature.

Life is daring all our human stature.
Death looks, and waits for each bright eye.
Love and harmony are our best nurture.
The human being is a lonely creature.

SESTINA

I die, no matter what I do I die.
Is this the sum of what man has to do?
There is no use to fly to be at ease.
Man flies, but knows not what he does.
It is in war you want to be in peace.
In Heaven, in Heaven I want to be in Hell.

The mortal span to find out Heaven and Hell!
No matter what I have to do I die,
The gods comply to cancel you to peace.
Before this then what is it man should do?
And after, does it matter what he does?
Will Christ-like Christ then put him at his ease?

Will will will him his own, a fabled ease?
Will, some say, is the whole road to Hell.
But man is bound to Hell whatever he does.
No matter what he does he has to die.
It is the dying that you have to do
Defies the hyaline lustre of the peace.

Despair has not the end in view of peace
Nor has desire the purposes of ease,
But action, while you live, is what's to do.
Thought is three crossed roads that lead to Hell,
Your thought is fatal and will make you die,
For thinking kills as much as action does.

It is not what he thinks, nor what he does
Nor what cold mystery of the Prince of Peace
Avails—no matter what I do I die,
May nothing, nothing put me at my ease
Except the reality of Heaven and Hell.
No one told me what I ought to do.

The scriptures told you what you ought to do.
They are unreasonable truth, and what man does
Believe when most he believes in Heaven and Hell.
That passes understanding, that is peace.
But sky-fallen man will not be put at ease.
I die, no matter what I do I die.

No matter what I do I have no peace.
No matter what man does he has no ease.
Heaven and Hell are changeless when I die.

ON THE FRAGILITY OF MIND

Mind is a most delicate evidence.
Not a soul has seen it yet.
And yet I think it is dense,
Although of great expense.

I suspect it of all trickery,
The master of the greatest paradoxes.
It is the historian of the world,
Crafty and foxy.

Old entablatures in Venice remind me
Of the mind of Tintoretto or Veronese.
These came to a watery nothingness
But for the golden paint I see.

I think there is no mind at all,
Perhaps, but only desires and faiths,
And the great capability of art
Which shows us forms, divine.

THE BOOK OF NATURE

As I was reading the book of nature
In the fall of the year
And picking the full blueberries
Each as round as a tear;

As I was being in my boyhood
Scanning the book of the rocks,
Intercepting the wrath to come
Where the hay was in the shocks;

As I was eye-drinking the waters
As they came up Seal Cove
With the eyes of my dazzled daughter,
An absolutist of a sudden grove;

As I was on that sea again
With islands stretching off the sail,
The real sea of mysterious time,
Islands of summer storm and hail;

As I was living with the love of death,
A concentrated wonder of the birches,
Passionate in the shudder of the air
And running on the splendour of the waters;

As I was a person in the sea birds,
And I was a spirit of the ferns,
And I was a dream of the monadnocks,
An intelligence of the flocks and herds;

As I was a memory of memory,
Keeper of the holy seals,
The unified semblance of disparates
And wielder of the real;

As I was happy as the ospreys,
As I was full of broom and bright afflatus,
As I was a vehicle of silence
Being the sound of a sudden hiatus;

As I was the purified exemplar
And sufferer of the whole adventure,
And as I was desire in despair,
A bird's eye in doom's nature;

As I stood in the whole, immaculate air,
Holding all things together,
I was blessed in the knowledge of nature.
God is man's weather.

Then I saw God on my fingertip
And I was glad for all who ever lived,
Serene and exalted in mood,
Whatever the mind contrived.

Then God provided an answer
Out of the overwhelming skies and years
And wrath and judgment then and there
Shook out the human tears.

COUSIN FLORENCE

There it is, a block of leaping marble
Given to me by an ancestor.
The hands that passed it held down ninety years.
She got it in the love-time of Swinburne.

This woman with her stalwart mien,
More like a Roman than a Greek,
Fumbled among old bags of rubble
For something indomitable that she could seek.

She saw the light of ancient days around her,
Calling in the hip-cracked hospital.
She chose at last. Then the clear light
Of reason stood up strong and tall.

With a pure, commanding grace
She handed me a piece of the Parthenon,
Saying, this I broke with my own hands,
And gave me the imagination of the Greeks.

I thought the spirit of this woman
The tallest that I had ever seen,
Stronger than the marble that I have,
Who was herself imagination's dream

By the moment of such sacrament,
A pure force transmitting love,
Endurance, steadfastness, her calm,
Her Roman heart, to mine, of dream.

I would rather keep her noble acts,
The blood of her powerful character, a mind
As good as any of her time, than search
My upward years for such a stone that leaps.

ANALOGUE OF UNITY IN MULTEITY

A man of massive meditation
Is like a man looking at death,
Looking at death as at a bull's-eye.
He watches before he crosses the tracks.

Every day a man is in a box,
Hourly he watches the trains go by,
Opening and closing the wooden gates,
As one who is interested in the world.

The man who is massive in thought,
As it were of mountainous fortitude,
Whom decades have seasoned in male beauty,
Whose clarity is an age of harmony,

A man of intellectual power
Will not be killed by a ribboned artifice.
He is too full of deaths to be undone,
Death is his hourly communion.

Who will say what the gate-keeper thinks?
A man necessary to the metropolis,
Comfort he knows, he keeps a comfort station,
As decades pass on shining steel.

The meditative man, a power of eye,
Big shouldered, with the torso of a Jove,
Is master of a world of action,
An actor in a world of masks.

In complex thought he walks along
The most fearless man to be seen,
For with animal nature he is one,
Who looks ever death in the bull's-eye.

Far in the sky another eye
Beholds these creatures in their ways,
Indifferent to their differences,
A point of agate reference.

TO EVAN

I wanted to give him some gift,
The breath of my breath, the look of my eyes,
I wanted to give him some gift,
Lying there so piteously.

I wanted to give him some gift,
Small child dying slowly,
With brave blue intelligent eyes,
His form withered piteously.

Only in the intelligence of those eyes
Where life had retreated for a piercing look
Was the enormous mystery justified,
As he inhaled the betraying oxygen.

I wanted to give him some gift,
A look from my look not to frighten him,
A breath from my haleness, my even vigour,
The same breath as his lonely breath.

Tenacious life in this little form
That will soon vanish from it entirely,
Unforgettable features of this little boy,
Do you mock my passion in your long passing?

I wanted to give him some gift,
Breath of my breath, the look of my eyes,
This is all upon earth, under heaven,
I can give him, a child dying, and I unwise.

Though I would menace the tall skies
And cry out as man has from the beginning
At the unequal fate held over us from our birth
I could not for a moment suspend this child's dying.

O though I would look into his intelligent eyes
With the world's weight of experience and despair
I could not mate the black look before death,
Nor seize the secret from the secrecy.

I wanted to give him some gift,
Breath of my breath, the look of my eyes.
Farewell, fair spirit. Fare forward, voyager.
I pass away silently and see him no more.

FORMATIVE MASTERSHIP

Never be happy until the golden hour
Creates its living death upon the instant
Just beyond perception: be happy then,
That you shall never understand that radiant
Mastery. It is gone as soon as known,
Known only as a breath of incalculable spirit,
Wordless peak except verbs prick at it;
Perhaps never known, but in this mating time.

Never be broken by the things of evil
That pass upon the years to true forgetfulness,
Giving themselves back to nature; man's evil
Forget, for in time forget you must,
Whether man wrought them from his crooked heart,
Or life imposed them in a cruel majesty
Impersonal and blind. Do not shake the fist
Or cry the brutal rage: time heals the time.

Baffled by instances of malice, keep
The calm of solitary imaginings,
That harmony inhere although the flesh be maimed,
Keep struggle pure with a white intent,
Revising possibility. Pare the naked nature
And in dark hours accept what fate is.
What toys we are to crippling chance
When victim, not the callers, of a savage dance.

Look upon the passing scene with tenderness.
All suffers change. The blight is in the air,
Within the lungs, within the light, within
The eye. Great nature is our master.
All our will and our flushed, enticed brains
Cannot unmake the world. Talk to the night
When the woods are deep, the stars alight.
Talk out the long instancy of mankind.

THE DAY-BED

I

It is green, it is made of willow.
I am baffled: I cannot think about it.
An obsession of twenty-seven years.
I am brutalized to look upon it.

The very form of love. Of time
The essence, which is memory.
The flash of light, and a long sleep.
This is the bed of day, and night.

No, but soft, but untold love
Arises. The very heart of love!
So long ago that suffering form
Slowly grew to death through pain,

Here on this very furniture.
It seems impossible. Time lies.
I do not see her lying there,
Great eyes, great gray-black hair.

I do not see that agonizing stare
That's deep through all my nights and days,
Substratum of the flying years;
The great pain without a cure.

II

Reality is a passing thing.
The Day-Bed lives, remains, reminds
Of the eternity of change
To this same, writing finger.

The emblem remains, bounteous gift,
The strange, pure gift of memory,
A blooded drench, a flushed presentiment;
And throngs and throngs of images.

Day-Bed of Life-in-Death,
That while my eyes shall change and see,
I look upon this furniture,
The not estranging imagery.

And summon up the love, and see
The very form and flesh of love
As it is with all mankind,
The loves long lost, the loves most near.

Who cursed the blood within the veins
Appareling day with source of night
Shall dream upon a lovely dream
Though the deep heart choke, and fight.

III

It is green, it is made of willow.
Lithe winds of Spring wave over it.
It is a new time and a new day,
New flesh here springs in harmony,

Laughs and tumbles and is gay.
Is gay! Is lithe as wings of Spring
And bends to nature as a willow
Triumphing in its green, cool stay.

Two lovers here electing unity
Flaunt eclectic idols in the day,
Consuming the great world of sense,
And laughing in its careless sway.

They sway. They laugh. And leaping
Loosen the mind from iron prisons,
Celebrating speeds of instancy
In vernal cells of intimacy.

Green and willowy marriage time!
Time of the beliefless flesh!
Time of the charges of the ruddy blood,
Joy that is swift and free, pure joy.

IV

Other years and other foils
Requite the ancient mysteries,
Persuading of some subtle balance
Between the losing and the winning battles,

Here on this very furniture,
Day-Bed of Life-in-Death!
A child plays in boisterous industry,
Truth off the old bones of mating.

Embroiled in fate he does not know,
Smiling mischievous and saintly,
Evidently impossible to quell,
The very future in his active eye,

The willowy Day-Bed of past time
That taught death in the substratum
Couches now the bliss of man,
A bright shape, a green new dream.

SEA-HAWK

The six-foot nest of the sea-hawk,
Almost inaccessible,
Surveys from the headland the lonely, the violent waters.

I have driven him off,
Somewhat foolhardily,
And look into the fierce eye of the offspring.

It is an eye of fire,
An eye of icy crystal,
A threat of ancient purity,

Power of an immense reserve,
An agate-well of purpose,
Life before man, and maybe after.

How many centuries of sight
In this piercing, inhuman perfection
Stretch the gaze off the rocky promontory,

To make the mind exult
At the eye of a sea-hawk,
A blaze of grandeur, permanence of the impersonal.

ON A SQUIRREL CROSSING THE ROAD IN AUTUMN, IN NEW ENGLAND

It is what he does not know,
Crossing the road under the elm trees,
About the mechanism of my car,
About the Commonwealth of Massachusetts,
About Mozart, India, Arcturus,

That wins my praise. I engage
At once in whirling squirrel-praise.

He obeys the orders of nature
Without knowing them.
It is what he does not know
That makes him beautiful.
Such a knot of little purposeful nature!

I who can see him as he cannot see himself
Repose in the ignorance that is his blessing.

It is what man does not know of God
Composes the visible poem of the world.

              . . . Just missed him!

IN AFTER TIME

In after time, when all this dream
Becomes pure dream, and roughest years
Lie down among the tender grass,
And spring up sentient upon the meadow;

In that after time of great-born Aprils,
Beyond a century of tatters and of malice,
When love has thrown out fear and madness
The eyes will see the sun as wonder.

In after time, when rage and chaos
Lose their sovereign force, new dream
Will lift the shining life to spirit
And mate the make of man to merit.

Then shall holy summers come; then laughter
God-like shake upon a dewy morning;
Then fullness grow, big with purpose,
And man shall know again his richness.

THE WISDOM OF INSECURITY

The endless part of disintegration
Is that it will build again;

Of a robin,
That he will become a memory;

Of a hand-great August moth,
With eyes in his wings, so fine

As to represent himself as a fable,
That he will be tried again in a poem;

Of a petal-departed rose,
That it is its loving grandparents;

Of the evil of man to man,
That it is the tenacity of mankind

To put it out of mind in the long time
And commit to the heart new fidelities;

Of the broken music of silence,
That it will be brought together,

Renaming poetry; of the day's colours,
That they make the painter's paradigm;

Of immeasurable fallibility,
That it becomes art, by authority;

That the disintegration of time
Becomes the enrichment of timelessness,

So that nothing is destroyed, but finds
Its truth in the eternal mind;

That death provides nowise no escape.
Man becomes some other shape.

I must have come down from Adam
And am his metropolitan.

The leaves are falling and the rain.
Mystery is palpable. Sameness ever the same,

Ever different, where I look
Is through the fish to the fish-hook.

The strangeness of the poet's dream
Will set what is, not what seems.

When you see destruction itself
You see form out of the formless

As I recall in the Campo Santo, at Pisa,
The work of medieval Giovanni

Who painted an old man, prone and dead,
An infant, the soul, springing from his head.

ONLY IN THE DREAM

Only in the dream that is like sleep
When time has taken the measure of live things
By stark origination
Is mankind redeemed.

Only in the melancholy of the music
Of the midnight within the blood
Comes the fulfilment
After faring years.

Only in the balance of dark tenderness
When everything is seen in its purity
Do we penetrate
The myth of mankind.

Only in the mastery of love
Is anything known of the world,
Death put aside
With pure intent.

Only in the long wastes of loss
Comes the mystical touch on the brow
That triumph grow,
Insatiable, again.

ANIMA

We are betrayed by what is false. Within
Our hearts good and evil strive. Our minds,
Sometimes aloft, above grace, or sin,
Search out satisfaction. Time reminds

Our senses of the savage contradictions
Entertained tumultuously. We win,
We lose, we stay awhile upon convictions.
In some new century has any been?

The falsity is life itself. We are
Betrayed by time, which made us mortal. Time
Is a laughing light upon an ancient star.
Inmost thought is subtly made to rhyme.

It is the perdurable toughness of the soul
God and Nature make us want to keep;
The struggle of the part against the whole.
Each time we take a breath it must be deep.

THE FORGOTTEN ROCK

Tawny in a pasture by the true sea
Ship-shaped it stood, the never realizable
Rock.

It was the awe placed on this natural object,
When looking at one thing, another world was seen,
He remembered.

Even this rock, sun-stroked, high-fashioned,
Peopling dream, enticing him completely,
Was never itself.

With such subtlety the blood, blue-watery source,
Leaped from one thing to something other.
A double escape,

A paragon of sight was posed upon
The blue rock; the excitation of the world
Glanced off.

This was nothing but the world itself;
A voyage in blue distance under tawny charges
Vividly known,

As a ship like a jewel of sense, come to
With boundless appetite, is yet unknown,
And is forgotten,

As we forget time that is thoroughly gone,
But was so certainly there. We annihilate time
To remember,

And what we remember is the duality of time.
The rock was never known as it was,
But as we are.

It had a cave with an obscure dome
A hawk flew into heading home,
Killed instantly.

THE RETURN

Still marvelling at the light,
Impersonal, on the mountain peaks, a halcyon
Glow; it strains to me,
To the last intimacy.

Then, quick to seize on intuition,
I thought I knew; now I know
I do not know. Time has refracted
Ineluctable meanings.

Now, the sight is more satisfactory.
Decades make us mountainous.
Life did not know what time could do.
My long light streams out to you.

ATTITUDES

IRISH CATHOLIC

After the long wake, when many were drunk,
Pat struggled out to the tracks, seething
Blinded, was struck by a train,
Died too. The funeral was for the mother and son.

The Catholic music soared to the high stones,
Hundreds swayed to the long, compulsive ritual.
As the mourners followed the caskets out
Wave followed wave of misery, of pure release.

NEW ENGLAND PROTESTANT

When Aunt Emily died, her husband would not look at her.
Uncle Peter, inarticulate in his cold intelligence,
Conceded few flowers, arranged the simplest service.
Only the intimate members of the family came.

Then the small procession went to the family grave.
No word was spoken but the parson's solemn few.
Silence, order, a prim dryness, not a tear.
We left the old man standing alone there.

LIGHT FROM ABOVE

The vigor and majesty of the air,
Empurpled in October, in an afternoon

Of scudding clouds with sun breaking through,
Showing a militant light on mountain and river,

Is the imperial power
Greater than man's works

I praise and sing; my headlong delight
In unsymbolic gestures of eternity;

For here, surely, above the worn farms,
Their stoical souls and axe patience,

Whatever man learned from the soil, from
Society, and from his time-locked heart,

Is the greater, the grand, the impersonal gesture
And the imperial power; here, the great sky,

Full of profound adventure beyond man's losses,
Tosses the locks of a strong, abrasive radiance

From the beginning, and through the time of man,
And into the future beyond our love and wit,

And in the vigor and majesty of the air
I, empurpled, think on unity

Glimpsed in pure visual belief
When the sky expresses beyond our powers

The fiat of a great assurance.

NOTHING BUT CHANGE

We saw nothing but change in all the ways we went,
Nothing but time weaving wind, weaving the willows,
The tall buildings taken down and put up again
As we looked at them; the bridges made again.

We beheld the same of persons, nothing but change,
A kind of personal constancy we thought it to be.
Inured, we finally felt when somebody died
It was part of the flow of time, the nature of ourselves.

Then time itself began to get the upper hand
As our bodies, falling to the stress of air,
Left us to ridicule; Plato and Christ were bare.
A life-time of thought could not get through the flesh

And all the pledges of superlative intellect,
The rich, sensuous breasts of memory,
Fictions of the spirit, whips of the blood
Met denial, the unanswerable, God-given death;

    The veritable and very rich death,
    Without a poem, riches itself,
    And when the gaudy play was enacted,
    It was all a roundness, all a poetry.

THE OAK

    Some sway for long and then decline.
    There are those, a very few,
    Whose rings are golden, hard, and just,
    Like a solid oak all through.

Each year builds on another truth,
A suffering, a joy increased in gold.
You cannot see, viewing the edifice,
Whether it is young or old.

Some have it in them to keep close
To nature, her mysterious part,
Seeming strange to be so natural,
Nature married to perfected art.

Flesh will ponder its dark blame.
Mind will never mate the true.
But the whole being will rejoice,
Like a solid oak all through.

THE INCOMPARABLE LIGHT

The light beyond compare is the light I saw.
I saw it on the mountain tops, the light
Beyond compare. I saw it in childhood too.
I glimpsed it in the turbulence of growing up.
I saw it in the meshes of meaning of women.
I saw it in political action, and I saw
The light beyond compare in sundry deaths.

Elusive element, final mystery,
The light beyond compare has been my visitant,
Some sort of angel sometimes at my shoulder,
A beckoning guide, elusive nevertheless,
Under the mind where currents of being are running,
It is this strange light I come back to,
Agent of truth, protean, a radical of time.

The light beyond compare is my meaning,
It is the secret source of my beginning,
Issuance of uniqueness, signal upon suffering,

It is the wordless bond of all endings,
It is the subtle flash that tells our song,
Inescapable brotherhood of the living,
Our mystery of time, the only hopeful light.

OSPREYS IN CRY

When I heard the call of the osprey,
The wild cries of the ospreys
Breasting the wind high above
The cliff, held static
On updraft over the ocean,
Piercing with ancient, piercing eyes
The far ocean deep

I felt a fleshed exultance
For the fierce, untamed beauty
Of these sea-birds, sea-hawks,
Wild creatures of the air,
Magnificent riders
Of the wind's crests, plummeters
Straight down for prey

Caught under water in talons
Triumphant as life,
The huge birds struggling up
Shaking heavy water off
And powerfully taking the air
With fish in talons head first;

I felt a staggering sense
Of the victor and of the doomed,
Of being one and the other,
Of being both at one time,
I was the seer
And I was revealed.

BIRTH AND DEATH

I dropped to depth,
And then I leaped to height,
But in between was the fearsome place.

All imaginative skill
Could not shape the in between,
While depth and height were absolute.

I called in philosophy,
With mortarboard on top, to help;
The serious gambit of wisdom.

And I called on love,
Great bounce, good thrall,
Knowing the happiness of lovers.

And action called on me,
Saying, take the sea, the sky;
Yours is the enthusiasm.

It was like the drama
Of a man thinking he
Could outwit life itself,

Like the search for purity,
Irrational struggle of the will,
A might and power and force.

The in between will not be conquered
So long as man shall strive
And struggle with the world.

I dropped to depth,
And then I leaped to height,
But in between was the fearsome place.

APPLE BUDS

Apple buds will never bloom
But to remind me of her room,
Impersonally proffering
Spring, when she was suffering.
She cannot take them in her hand
Again. I cannot understand
Her suffering, her suffering.
It is brutality to sing.

A COMMITMENT

I am committed
To the spirit that hovers over the graves.

All greatness flails.
Even evangelical Aristotle

Deploys his systems into mysticism,
Obfuscating his clarity of sight.

Plato goes with us on a picnic
As we mammock our hamburgers.

The logic of illogic,
The illogic of logic plays through time.

Poetic justice
Still is to get what we deserve.

I dream, here, now
Of the two-faced caprice of poetry,

Clarity of day,
Ambiguous necessities of night.

A spirit hovers
Over the stars, and in the heart.

Love is long
And art is good to stitch the time.

THE KITE

I *Sensitivity of the First Flight*

Your blood has coursed and rushed with anticipation.
You have studied the ratcheted wheels of the reel,
Invested yourself in the rig of the parachute-like harness,
Learned bowline, fisherman's bend, four-strand overhand, larks-
    head loop.
Already many times tangled in the winding drums
You have exercised exegetical practice on the lines,
Threaded and rethreaded spanwise the spreader bar,
If need be with a twig or straw, by the sea's edge.

II *Theory*

Not like that example showing the absolute mastery of nature
So that if there is wind enough to lift the lovely shape
The same wind turning a vane at the fore
Turns with remitted motion a rudder at the rear,
So back and forth, to right and left, across the sky
Steered by its own motion, the sail must go

With a low, long undulation of precision
Standing into the sky with a sublime indifference
And regularity to the whims that may destroy it,

As if it were its own theory and reason for being
Freely the agent of its own pleasing exercise,
Imperturbable before the wind's perturbation,
Nicety, balance and ease of operation; as if
There were order in the universe; as if
Order were in the mind of man,
But as everything is fixed to something
So this air-engine, in an access of cleverness,
Itself moving in azimuth or elevation
Is fixed to light metal rods in the shape of an A,
This fixation the more to unfix our earthless emblem,
For the wind that keeps aloft the sail
And equally sails it slowly to and fro,
The vane being attached by linen cords to the A,
Also deftly marches it on the surface of the ocean,
This free and faultless thing then is a target,
Can be launched from cruiser or battleship,
Will make a deflection target for air gunnery,
Can be shot at by different ships in passing,
The metal floats so cunningly devised
That upon destruction in the air by gunfire,
Or descent of the sail for lack of air-power,
A change of weights and balances opens small holes,
The sea rushes in, the whole engine sinks from sight
Leaving no trace to enemies upon the broad Pacific,
As a dream kept long alive, aloft, in night thoughts
Suddenly disappears from the mind beyond any call.

To be a flier of kites is not the least of my desires!
In this you see the symbol of your relation to the universe;
The wind, unseen, is God, upon which all is dependent,
Sometimes absent, sometimes present, always possible,
In time. The sail, whether in guise of cerulean
Blue make, undistinguishable at a distance from the sky,
Or almost so, as you are from nothingness, in time,
Or almost so, is soul or spirit, yours,
Which you release to flight, which seems to be free,

But over which you hold manoeuverability
Yet it is nothing without the Author of its motion;
Or dotted like a Hamp, a Tony, a Rufe, or Nan
Its suns of rising redness set before the sun's gold eye,
Held thus in the sky to be a mask, the sign of evil,
And save your eye from the true sun's all-inclusiveness,
Else dazzling you, the sun not truly masked,
You lose control, all's gone in a second to wreckage.

If you would look into the sun, put something before it,
Put the mask of evil before it if you can.

Or say the sky is the father-mother symbol, the
Wind is the generator, the lines umbilical,
And you the kite: Fly high, fly low, luff
Or porpoise, or buckle, or break your bonds,
Whether destroyed in the ocean, or destroyed on the sand,
You are not lost, but a part of the world's plan.
It is the sperm searching the great womb of the sky,
Restless with creative energy, flirting with eternity,
Attempting the gift of itself beyond itself,
Dying upon the very air that holds it up,
Pulled down by the harness and the reel.
So our thoughts would transcend themselves
But they are limited to the human.
So our souls would unite with God,
But they are imprisoned by the body.
And our intelligences ever at great play
Assume a certain lightness through the years!
Our wills finally respond to the controls
Of infinite forces as viewless as the wind.

III   *The First Flight, and Later*

Then you carry the great thing down to the sea,
To the sand by the sea, harnessed, weighted with gear,
Your helper-launcher eager as you.

In a basket an extra spool of linen string,
A knife, pliers, broad Scotch tape, and a metal box
Brimful of buttons, screw eyes, nuts and bolts, the hardware:
You are the wind's guesser, a neophyte of this element
Searching a distant flagpole, or smoke, or leaves swishing.

With care the bowing is accomplished, all conditions
According to the book are fulfilled, she stands
Taut and singing and a living thing.
On the broad beach, with gulls and hawks playing
And far above airplanes making other curvets
Now the helper walks with it backward
Two hundred feet as you reel out the double lines,
Your hand on the reel-brake to keep the lines taut.
Then holding it up as the arms will,
The helper obliterated by the enormous emblem before,
You test the lines for equal tension,
With horizontal motion of the flying bar
Flap the rudder, when all is ready
As you think, and you are all wary, signal "Up Sail."
Straight up with grace incomparable rising
To high center the kite goes sailing and shining.
In your heart and in your hands are triumph.
Long care you have exercised, long patience,
And you think you have cunning.
Such contending as this is in the unpredictable.
The high quiring! Classless you are clumsy,
In a trice it loops over and crashes down,
Instantly inert; broken on the beach.

Quickly dashed this sail, delicate as sensation.

Inspecting the wreckage, you search the cause.
Was it lack of knowledge, or the wind's cantankerous veer?
Then you excise the broken spar, put in a spare,
Make with greater caution and wariness another attempt.

The second time she goes up ten feet
Whirls over and is dashed to pieces in sand.
Again you make necessary repairs,
Baffled by the testy, bluffy bird.

The flier will practice by the hour, and achieve
Slowly the relaxed ease of his controlling motions,
Slowly he will learn the habits of the sail's tactics,
And soon respects the grandeur of the wind's potentiality.

With diligence, the hours flying away in exhilaration
The flier will learn the secret of anticipation
So that the unforeseeable future of the kite's motion
Is the guide of the present instant's motivation;
Unless this is accomplished disaster is imminent!

Then the dominating shape, sturdy in the sky,
Well-weathered and living in its keen nature,
Responsive to the controlled will of the flier
Will be seen to make slow arcs across
The sky's quarter, or hover far over into
The wind, slowly descending, or will rush
Up bright to high center, or be compelled
Crabwise across to its last inch of wind-take,
Or perform complete circles to right or left,
Or dazzle the eye in a spectacular figure eight,
Lastly even diving from zenith to,
Almost to earth! reseated upward
Even ten feet before seeming crash to earth
By dexterous, subtle motion of the flying bar!

Much depends upon how much throat you give it,
How it will fly. The slightest adjustment
Of the larkshead loop, will tell. What I call
Open-throated rides against the wind,
Is best in a thirty knot wind for power dives,

But close-throated turns less face to the wind,
Rides more nearly atop it, is gentle sailing,
But that it comes almost overhead porpoising
Which, then, compels correction.

It is possible to dispense with the reel,
To go with no harness, by primitive means
For a flight, having constructed a stick,
Even a broomstick, as a flying bar,
One linen line attached to each end,
The strings wound around as on a bobbin.
This gives for quicker action than the other,
The kite is harder to control, more adventuresome to fly,
Will outhand you in an instant
If you are not continuously concentrating;
Is hard to bring in, but with lucky skill
Can be landed by a forward rush to drop it.

IV   *The Wind as an Abstract God*

Every day one looks for the signs of the wind,
Which has now become a living thing, obsessive,
Thought of in terms of sail-lifting pleasure,
A rustle in the holly trees; will it be
Enough? The flag is always indicating,
At the Cavalier. Often in excess of elan
You have tromped all your gear down to the beach
In the anticipation of eight knots, or
Taken the smooth seven-footer that will sail in six,
Its pale blue cover to go slowly and stately,
But by this token it is also less manoeuverable.

Your knowledge of the wind was faulty, and even
Though there is wind at the edges of the waves
Your helper lifts aloft, and you reel in hard,
But the kite will not rise, falling, unbroken.

The fascination of the thing is in the wind!

Sometimes sailing, the kite well exercising,
The wind will drop, and nothing can be done,
Nothing, nothing.
You go, with all your gear, reluctant, home.

And you had learned obedience to nature,
Desirous man, had learned obedience to nature,
Before you sulked home with your sticks and fabrics.

V   *Adventure on Sunday*

By the seashore, by the Hotel Splendide
When days were on the flame, but lessening
And would not kill the skin with stings,

But far enough away, quite far away,
But by the house that read "No Trespassing,"
Not once, but each ten feet upon the jetty,

That house that held a terrible old lady
Whom Furies drove to such a loneliness
She picked up sticks upon the sand all day,

By dawn, and equally in amber evening
She'd rake the sand for any obstacles
But sand, by hand, upon her eminent domain,

Yet dawn the sea dragged in obstreperous foray
And night would overwhelm her restless energy
With wreckage, sea's greenery, a lungfish, a great booby.

Then retreating farther down the beach
In an access of politic prehension,
A pontiff wind available, you come

To the tasks of assembly and adjustment,
Of balancing, and testing, and pre-correction,
To attempt the launching of the vane alone.

By resting the sail on its side on the sand
It is possible to run out the lines, then even them
And reel in until pressure brings it edge up.

Then with swift reel-in off she takes
Laterally and if adroitly handled evenly
Crabs across up and soon seeks high center.

The wind now ardent, you reel out
Letting the wind take it, back, until flapping,
Then put on the brakes to tauten it up.

Then let her go again in opulence of motion
The plane growing smaller, shrinking bright,
And still you let it out, and out, and out,

Noting the gradual slowing of the controls,
The time-lapse in the reaction of the strings
As these gleam deep, in deep unequal curves

Flashing white against the blue, but lost far up.
And you are strong in a springy disrelation
Almost divorced from the plane you control.

It must be almost over the Hotel Splendide!
It must be out almost two hundred yards.
It is tugging on the harness, lustily,

When, pong! the plane loops down under
In a huge circle, comes up, loops over,
Begins another descent, you reel in, run back,

She barely comes up, she goes up over,
Something has snapped, you try for control,
She goes way down under, the thing is giddy,

You barely get her up, each circle losing
Altitude, is altogether behaving crazily,
You reel in frantically. O way down

She goes, she has gone way way down
Out of sight behind the terrible lady's house,
Both lines are hung up over the roof.

It would be the "No Trespassing" house!
Friends come; all assess the situation.
Strangers appear, gazing at the strange gear.

It is not an inconsiderable problem,
The lines are caught hard on the roof. Will
Anybody appear, from the house? You seriously care.

Eventually a sort of council of war.
Actually a calculation of strategy
Upon an attempt at the extravagant.

Another five-footer is put together.
Will the wind hold? Will it work?
Every effort to free the lines has failed.

The reel is wound in to the edge of the lot,
The lines just taut to the top of the roof.
The new kite is held by its delicate bridle,

Each end of the bridle secured to a reel-line
And the idea is to fly the fouled lines off!
"Up Sail." Up she goes heavy and cranky

Carrying the burden of the lines beyond her,
Seeming to refuse, but rising queerly,
Now at the housetop, and now higher rising

The stuck lines are lifted gently away
The useful kite then steered to the beach,
Landed safely to the delight of beholders.

Before which the Jap was thrashing around in the parking lot,
Illogical plaything of partial-fitting wind,
Restrained by dead lines fixed to the roof.

High in air, a tiller-line snapped out a spar eyelet

VI *Aerialism*

A whole day of sailing is delight!
Or a day of intermittent sailing and lazing,
For you can find a cove among the dunes
Back a distance from the surf's gift,
In broad view of the expansive Atlantic,
For the repair of kites, or rest between ventures,
With friends, or alone. All day the wind tussles,
Or sometimes it will sink for an hour,
Or rise puffy: there, shielded, on tan grass
Pointed inland by months of wind-rush,
You study the texture of the sail's make,
Rig the lines, attend to checks and balances,
Repair a rent with Scotch tape, barefoot.

To sail by the sea pleases inly
When the wind comes onto the shore
In great staves like music
Playing against your muscles to the orchestrated,
Intricately shifting movements of the vane.
Then it is to test the far-out motion,

Facing to the South, to fly the lines over,
To fly the kite out over the ocean,
Four hundred feet out, say, the wind
Sagging the lines between you and it,
So that there is a certain peril in the control
By time-lapse; also the edge of the wind
May endanger, by lack of its steadiness,
The intrusive tactic into the wind.

By now tipped over, the mast almost horizontal,
You edge it up wind as far as it will go,
With skill try to keep it motionless and still,
Then, with a sense of shearing the minimum,
By forcing it just to horizontal, O be deft,
Down almost to the very touch of the waves
You love to let it.

If disaster results, you rush to the scene,
Try to catch the swamped bird on the in-come,
It must be caught before the last breaker
For the last breaker invariably breaks it up.

Then another attempt of similar aviation.
This time more safely not over the ocean,
You try, by the same minute hand motions,
Trying to gauge errors of the wind's differential,
To land the kite upwind on the beach.
Often like the most skittery bird,
Impatient as a spirit, an earthless thing.
"Light as the wind," the lithe being of the kite
Will dance with an enthralling delicacy,
Just at the touch, or less than touch, of the sand,
Straining and quivering to be up, flirting,
A creature of the completest absence of mind,
An elemental spirit, soul of the graceful.

Then a practiced hand, tightening the controls,
Can bring the full vigor of upward compulsion.

Evening flight makes evening an advancer,
Too soon an all darkener. But you stand there
When you can hardly see what you are doing,
O metaphysical adventure!

Until the moon arises,
And you can mask it.

O strange and impalpable evanescence
To be flying by the light of the moon,
With dark-adapted eyes, but uncertain
At any instant what your relation
To the sail is, or how to maintain it,

As it is always with us and reality,
In the eccentric heart of philosophy,

Surely this supposition of control
Yet without certainty of the control

Is where nature has us,
And we have set our minds

For centuries up in the heavens
Where they fly, secreted, dark,

Riding on the winds of chance.

LA CROSSE AT NINETY MILES AN HOUR

Better to be the rock above the river,
The bluff, brown and age-old sandstone,
Than the broad river winding to the Gulf.

The river looks like world reality
And has the serenity of wide and open things.
It is a river of even ice today.

Winter men in square cold huts have cut
Round holes to fish through: I saw it as a boy.
They have a will to tamper with the river.

Up on the high bluffs nothing but spirit!
It is there I would be, where an Indian scout was
Long ago, now purely imaginary.

It is a useless and heaven-depended place,
Commodious rock to lock the spirit in,
Where it gazes on the river and the land.

Better to be rock-like than river-like;
Water is a symbol will wear us all away.
Rock comes to the same end, more slowly so.

Rock is the wish of the spirit, heavy symbol,
Something to hold to beyond worldly use.
I feel it in my bones, kinship with vision,

And on the brown bluffs above the Mississippi
In the land of my deepest, earliest memories,
Rushing along at ninety miles an hour,

I feel the old elation of the imagination.
Strong talk of the river and the rock.
Small division between the world and spirit.

THE PLACE

I

Eventually one finds
There is no environment
Patent for the poetic.

Any place will do.
Alas! One thought of a gold
Hullabaloo, a place of glass

Refinement with subtleties
Crossing the transparency
As lively as mind's images.

One thought of a vast portico
With appropriate, energized
Gods and beings, rich purposes.

Alas! Any place will do.
There is no poetical place,
America continues its practices.

Final toughness of the word,
The word bawling imperfections,
Its paradox to be heard.

II

There used to be
The violent struggle
For place, the right

Place poetic in countries
Or cities or underground,
The right place

Was thought emergent
And to harbor you,
Hello! Poetry Place.

The subconscious was
Nearest, perhaps dearest,
Anyway sheerest

But always fleering off.
Ways you went! Allurement
In echoic happiness.

There was no place for poetry.
Entrenched, my flesh is
Poetry's environment.

KAIRE

If I were Sophocles, brave with truth,
Writhing in the darkness of humanity,
Bright with an occluded brightness,
Able to hold in total mind
The fantastic reality of the human condition,
I wonder what I would have done
About a world beyond the Greek,
For he knew the zenith and nadir
Of passion, and he knew that beyond reality
Was the other passion of mythology,
That myths were sensual as tears or dreams,
The stains of error in the habit of truth,
Leaning beyond the flesh to the strength of the gods.

If I were Sophocles, ebullient and melancholy
Today, I would be unable to say
How far distant is the dream of Eros,

How divorced from primal concern seems truth,
How love is the power we but dimly see,
Love is that wholeness of the passionate mind
Glimpsed in the sensitivity of being;
The blind in our day see more than the seeing;
This is as the vessel in the enriching breeze
Knowing only immediately where the wind is blowing,
Yet time will take it to the mark
Eventually. Hear the lark
In its cry at dawn. Hear the stating
Breakers: before destruction they preserve you
To dream on a world of immortality.

THE STRUGGLE

Longing went out from him like a flag
Run up the mast of heavens. Rains were torn
From tremendous downpours. The careening ships
Strode in the chaos of the moral seas.
Everything
Was what it is not.

In the blasts of heavenly conjecture,
Maledictions crashing like tined thunderbolts,
The skies opened as in better centuries;
Mercy appeared, white-throated, visionary.
All would
Become what it is not.

Desire was against imperishable death,
A seed-bursting openness, an avenging
Unquenchable archangel, militant, consuming
The ether. Heaven defend the earth. All care
That love
Become what it is not.

NEXUS

The dead are hovering on the air,
So real they have their flesh and bones.
They appear as they had been,
And speak with firm, daytime tones.

I say, I cannot believe your power.
Go back into the ancient times.
The sun burns on my forehead now,
And thought comes in a spring of rhymes.

My love is like the blue of the air,
My son and daughter play at games.
We live in a yoked immediacy,
Imagination come, that no one tames.

Everything I do today
Moves with a stealthy, spirit strength,
A thrust into the future order,
But yet it has a backward length.

The dead are playing about my head
As real as present, effable air.
They have their power to make and shape
Each breath I take, each thought today.

A MAINE ROUSTABOUT

He was there as the yachts went by

Percy is my name; my accent is good,
I am told, as good as that of an Elizabethan.
I had no schooling beyond the age of sixteen.
My wife left me. I took to drink, live with a dog.
I resent children unless they can hold their own

With grown-ups. I've been around the world on ships,
Down Connecticut way on jobs, once got to Georgia,
Always return to the rocks and the hard times
Of Maine. At clambakes in the summertime
I sit with the summer folk on the conglomerate shore,
Play my old fiddle a sharp tune or two,
Old airs I learned from my brother when we were boys.
It was always tough with me. Sharp as the city folks
I think I am, but am ever wary against them,
Keep my difference, and will not let them tell me off.
I have no respect for their savage villainies,
Yet their power over life always fascinated me.
They own the place. They come and go, I'm left
To chores and dung. But I can catch a mackerel
Almost any afternoon on the incoming tide
With an old hook, when they're running, old line,
In my old boat: they won't take hook from the richlings.
If I scare the children with my grizzled face
It's an old gut forced with whiskey keeps me going.

SEA BURIAL FROM THE CRUISER *REVE*

She is now water and air,
Who was earth and fire.

Reve we throttled down
Between Blake's Point and Western Isle,

Then, oh, then, at the last hour,
The first hour of her new inheritance,

We strewed her ashes over the waters,
We gave her the bright sinking

Of unimaginable aftermaths,
We followed her dispersed spirit

As children with a careless flick of wrist
Cast on the surface of the sea

New-cut flowers. Deeper down,
In the heavy blue of the water,

Slowly the white mass of her reduced bones
Waved, as a flag, from the enclosing depths.

She is now water and air,
Who was earth and fire.

THE INWARD ROCK

When I had withdrawn into the uniqueness of rock
I assumed the inwardness of time.
I became rock: I was the rock and time
Living in pure events of eloquence.

I left great Caesar in the market place,
And heard the tyrants rise and fall
In jubilations of clashed syllables
That had no meaning at all.

Philosophers appeared to me in a dream
Whose advent made a pleasing sound;
Poets with their grave, synthetic eyes
Amazed the fronds to leap and bound.

The old hermit of Cape Rosier came
Who seventy years had stood at ease
By the side of the sea, with two black cats;
Saints finally smote him to his knees.

And that blind man who wove wicker chairs
All through the black and winter nights
To whom the world was as a peace
No others knew in their delights.

These appeared to possess the world,
And then a golden child of nine or ten
With light step under a golden head
Danced into the world of men.

But I had withdrawn into the uniqueness of the rock
Who sought impossible credulities.
I was rock and time: I had denied
The world to find poetic certainties.

So in the gift of silence, like the earth
Stable and defined in hardness and size,
I ventured into imaginative freedom,
In mystery, where truth is surprise.

FLUX

The old Penobscot Indian
Sells me a pair of moccasins
That stain my feet yellow.

The gods of this world
Have taken the daughter of my neighbor,
Who died this day of encephalitis.

The absentee landlord has taken over Tree Island
Where one now hesitates to go for picnics,
Off the wide beach to see Fiddle Head.

The fogs are as unpredictable as the winds.
The next generation comes surely on,
Their nonchalance baffles my intelligence.

Some are gone for folly, some by mischance,
Cruelty broods over the inexpressible,
The inexorable is ever believable.

The boy, in his first hour on his motorbike,
Met death in a head-on collision.
His dog stood silent by the young corpse.

Last week, the sea farmer off Stonington
Was tripped in the wake of a cruiser.
He went down in the cold waters of the summer.

Life is stranger than any of us expected,
There is a somber, imponderable fate.
Enigma rules, and the heart has no certainty.

RUBY DAGGETT

She, a woman of abrupt features,
Cocked an eye this way and that. Another
Decade went by. She sat still in her place,
Looking out at the alley from the bookstore.
She was the mistress of rich indices.
Who came, who went, who was in, who was out
She noted, impersonal above the day's charges.
Chocorua jumped from the cliff, the cash register struck.
Another decade passed, she sat erect.
Before she knew it another would come and go.
She, a woman of abrupt features,
In a small space, looking out at the alley,

Encyclopedic among files, ensconced,
Let vision flow over the peaks of time
As over the mountains of imaginative reality,
Watching the people and books come and go.
Ledyard cut his canoe, carved an archipelago.
She was like a peak. She was distant,
Who was always present. She was stalwart,
Like mountain silence. And she knew,
Take care of the day and the day will take care of you.
Roosevelt rolled up a ramp at Marlborough.
Ike beamed. Kennedy rolled up his sleeves on the green.
She knew the scent of books, as intimate as age.
In ink she suspected a waft of sage.

HARK BACK

To have stepped lightly among European marbles
Dwelling in a pantheon of air;

To have altered the gods in a fact of being;

To have envisaged the marriage
Of everything new with the old,

And sprung a free spirit in the world

Is to have caught my own spirit
On a bicycle in the morning

Riding out of Paris,
Heading South.

My flesh felt so good
I was my own god.

THE LOST

Most intimate, most far, most ethereally near,
It is you I write to, without a name,
Nameless and evocative and purposeful, blear,
Whose infinite life I esteem and claim:

It is you I hold most clear and most dear,
Most evocative and forever most pure and sure,
You who were destroyed by the rams of a tear,
For whom psychoanalysis had no prayer, no cure:

It is you who will read this in misery
I write for, you who may survive the volt fates,
And read the evolution of your stormy essence
As vessels diced and tolled in watery estates:

It is you who have escaped essential vainglory
And you who have trapped a final triumph of pride
At whose side in the purity of this clamant word
At the world's verge and judgment I rise, I ride:

It is you who drowning now were green with hope,
Whose life burst like a flare and dropped from sky,
Whose attitudes I espouse dark-heartedly:
It is for an impossible cause I would die.

Nameless my love, my loves, my many esteems.
It is all who are broken, who are nameless and reviled
I speak for in a language of the stalwart and kind,
In the redemption of forgiveness, as grace is to be mild.

You who were the image of the human fate,
You who shook, and you who arose and tried,
Who remember the savage depths of the world,
I speak for, reach. You shall not have died

Until each human heart lives for love alone
And every human spirit is enriched, occulted, blessed
With the hidden inherent spirit of the godhead,
Imperishable as the spirit of the possessed.

It is then, when love is victor and conqueror,
That, relaxing my revolution and astonishment,
Nameless my love, my loves, my many esteems,
I shall the gall, the spleen relax, take back, and repent.

WINTER KILL

Word traps catch big bears in silence.
They hunt the woods for years in freedom,
Keeping the counsels of the bees and snows.
Then, once unwary, a foot is caught in a trap.
The big black mountain comes atumble down.

His picture is put in the local paper.
The expressionless hunter stands in sullen pride;
A small son touches the nose of the brute.
The gun rests easy by the icy carcass;
People come to stare at the winter kill.

I would have him noble on the mountain side,
Roaming and treading, untrapped by man.
Man kills him only half for meaning,
Half out of thoughtlessness. The steaks
Are passed around as tokens to the neighbors.

Word traps catch big bears another way
When the meaning is total. The way a poem prinks
Into the heart from a forest hill
Is to have it in words, but never to have it.
Which is to say it is elusive still.

A NEW ENGLAND BACHELOR

My death was arranged by special plans in Heaven
And only occasioned comment by ten persons in Adams,
    Massachusetts.
The best thing ever said about me
Was that I was deft at specifying trump.
I was killed by my father
And married to my mother
But born too early to know what happened to me,
And as I was an only child
I erected selfishness into a personal religion,
Sat thinking forty years saying nothing.
I observed all. I loved to drink gin,
Would not have thought to go farther
Into arcane episodes of the heavier drugs,
And, being New England, always remained sober.
However, I confess now, I was
Always afraid of women,
I don't know why, it was just the way it was,
I could never get very close to any woman.
Knowledge and intelligence allowed me
The grand rationalization of this; also, I respected
Delicacy, but would not go too far in any direction.
I thought I was a good man. I was.
I did not obstruct the state, nor religion,
But I saw through both and maintained my independence.
I kept my counsels among the learned.
My learning was more private and precious than worldly.
The world had no sense of the devious,
So my private vicissitudes were mine alone.

I say all this with a special sort of grace
For I avoided many of the pitfalls of fallen man
And while I did not have heroic size, the
Creative grandeur, or mastership of the mind
I earned my bread by cynicism alone,
And blow you all a kiss from the tomb.

A NEW ENGLAND VIEW: MY REPORT

The men of Vermont were aiming at New Hampshire.
The men of New Hampshire were aiming at Vermont.
In the middle was a deer forced into the river.
He looked to the right, to the left, frightened, swam
Down the middle of the Connecticut river,
On a cold day in occlusive December.

It was a sight for the gods to behold.
The irony of his power was lost on the creature.
He displayed a fearful sense of his plight.
The deer faced death by drowning or by shot.
The men did not dare to raise their sights.
Such was the condition of the animal kingdom.

AM I MY NEIGHBOR'S KEEPER?

The poetry of tragedy is never dead.
If it were not so I would not dream
On principles so deep they have no ending,
Nor on the ambiguity of what things ever seem.

The truth is hid and shaped in veils of error
Rich, unanswerable, the profound caught in plain air.
Centuries after tragedy sought out Socrates
Its inexplicable essence visits us in our lair,

Say here, on a remote New Hampshire farm.
The taciturn farmer disappeared in pre-dawn.
He had beaten his handyman, but no great harm.
Light spoke vengeance and bloodstains on the lawn.
His trussed corpse later under the dam
Gives to this day no answer, says I am.

DREAM JOURNEY
OF THE HEAD AND HEART

My head, so rarely rent
For all the rending time does me
Into a dreaming vortex went
To see what I could see.

I wanted to go down those steeps
Into a place of the unknown,
For surely, I thought, my head
Would save me with strong bone.

I went downward, circling wide
In cold, diminishing cones
Until, when far away from warmth,
I walked on bare and icy stones.

They were harsh but jewel-like, thrice
I tried to turn about and go
But the fascination of profundity
Urged me onward, swart and slow.

The strictures came with further travail
As inward came the walls and ribs,
More brilliant seemed the lights
In tossing, skeletal cribs

Illuminating darkness with strange rites
As my balked walk was probed.
Endlessly I seemed to stop
And now I was disrobed.

Head, ravenous intelligence,
Help me out of this thin place,
I cried, but nothing in the head
Caused radiance in the face

Until the heart, with pity of nothingness,
Woke in a dream of grace,
When I rose back into the world
On sufferance of the human race.

MOMENT OF EQUILIBRIUM
AMONG THE ISLANDS

The sea repeats itself in light flourishes,
The southwest breeze-up of the midday
Is a lavish presentiment of possible danger,
Coves beckon as waves attack the prow
And slip past in stubby frenzies of loss.
Then we dare the open ocean; the green swells
We ride over with thorough, lordly motion,
Lovers of wind, sun, and the world-turn horizon,
And seek a new island, with a small spit of sand.
The anchor holds; we climb through contorted woods
Up boulders to an old granite quarry, whose
Dark, green, still, fresh water refutes the ocean.

It is the moment of looking down to still water
From massed granite blocks pleases the soul
With the hardness and fantasy of the world,
Before we must try again the gripping buoyancy
Of the salt sea, whose profound depths
Appear only to the imagination, while eyes
Survey the fresh roads the vessel walks
In triumph of buoyancy, delicacy, and strength,
As a philosopher continuing in the essential.
Then standing to the westward-closing sun
As the wind dies and waves grovel to stillness,
We reach at nightfall the landfall buoy of home.

RAINSCAPES, HYDRANGEAS, ROSES
AND SINGING BIRDS

Rain thunderstorms over the Potomac, in Georgetown,
Descend blistering June to the coolest aftermath
Of birds clamant, wet roses burgeoning to open
And airplanes hungering for the skies again.

I could not call it landscape. It is too intimate.
Here the lush nature of the summer world
Reads a strength of vines into any doubt,
States nature is hale despite the canting absolute.

Call to the caterpillar in furry brevity,
To the heavy bee dramatic over the tigerlily,
To the cardinal stripped of every perfidy,
To the cocktail party glancing from the glasses

And say that rainscapes, hydrangeas, roses and
Singing birds parade a splendor of late afternoon
In June in fleshtime in the saunter of early summer.
Children propel their skyey laughter to the future.

I am the proliferation of nature,
Non-political, affirmative, tumultuous,
I am the rainscape, hydrangeas, the rose and
The singing bird and bard, triumphing tumescent

In this hour of the earthly Paradise.
Opulence is as indifferent as death itself.
I would rather be and sing this positive hour
Than groan in nightscape nightmare makeshift error. Now

The storm is lifting and the pale, late, subservient sun
Salutes the skies with a rosy, infallible glow
Of delicate and parson-haunted ineffable benediction
As I think of my days in the earth, memory long aglow.

HARDENING INTO PRINT

To catch the meaning out of the air
Yet have it inviolably there,
Life I mean, the glimpse of power, incomparable times
Of total splendor, the sudden exaltations,

Flash of a thrush, a rush of golden insight,
To be caught up in titanic light
As if one saw into the depths of things,
Yet averts the eye, to try yet further mysteries,

It is into this rich reservoir
Of knowing and unknowing I flash,
And shake high lightning spears of life
In the long combats of mortal strife,

Thrush song piercing human ills
With rigor and wrench so deep,
This glimpse is of an immaculate joy
Heart suffers for, and wishes to keep.

MEDITATION ONE

The body tires of the nonsense of the world.
Where is the sense?

In the cartwheel of my daughter.
In the football catch of my son.

In blackouts, doubts, inabilities, horrors.
In the very indeterminations of our sense.

The body tires, but the mind follows illusion.
The mind is indefatigable while the body lives.

It is the mind that conceives glory and cunning.
And soars aloft at the slightest, sweet promptings.

If I were to sing the mind, I would sing
The resolute assumptions of prime difficulties

And I would bless the eagle soaring in the heavens
From a predisposition to height and sun-likeness.

If there is a fiction of the flesh, a lassitude
Engendered by years of hoeing the earth,

Is there not an equal fiction of the mind
Pondering Plato and Aristotle, who said all between them,

Or so it is said in our time, a fiction of possession,
For how can we allow these old men to rule our garden,

And if there is a fiction of the body and of the mind,
Where then is reality? Is it at Harvard? At Lagos?

I in a baffled clarity of unassimilated absolutes,
Which is to say a pleasure of archaic riches,

Sense where we start again
After living in the confines and starts of nonsense.

We begin with the belief in a great mother,
The motherwater and ancient, grand indestructibility

Of birth-thrust, and in this mystery remaining alive
We are the eager champions of onrushing time

Which we take in arms like an irresistible lover,
And have the world as in our time. Then the dearth

Of nature easily assailing our senses confronts us
With the inevitable and fast-coming knowledge of death,

Perplexing to aspiration, and so deep a charge
As to acknowledge the essence of our being.

Then where shall we go? And to whom apply?
Who but to God the anchor of man's vanity,

For I have aforesaid our stability
In gardens of growth, and a wise insouciance,

But then we are perplexed in furtive enigmas,
Distracted in feats and assonances of fates,

And we, in the peregrine style of full acquiescence,
Engage furor, belay our dangerous drops,

And think we have Heaven indeed in hand,
Think we have Hell safely under our belts,

But to God we have incontestably to go,
We have to announce him as we pale in flesh,

And to His Son our Saviour bow knee and give service,
When in folly of mind we see the folly of mind.

The dogged New England American, trumped at last,
Has his hand taken by a god in the underbrush,

As it were, and has to admit glorious intrusion
On his own pain and comforts of the rational mind

And thus lean to poetry as a canorous canticle
And high diapason Godward sent, impelling him

To delicate, time-defeating elaborations
Of the deepest serenities of the heart and mind.

For of all we have learned in a life of effort
Most we have learned is that we know little,

While in natural humility, able to envy our senses,
We are yet able to see another point of view,

To worship the rose window of Palma de Mallorca,
Or be breathless before Ilaria del Caretto.

I began on nonsense and I end on sense,
Which is the wish of man to cultivate the world's garden,

Give the Devil his due, praise God for invented Heaven,
And hold to the end every last thing in view.

MEDITATION TWO

Style is the perfection of a point of view,
Nowise absolute, but held in a balance of opposites

So that for a moment the passage of time is stopped
And man is enhanced in a height of harmony.

He has purchased at a great price the gems of elan
In some avid precinct of his personality,

The price of years of doubt and belief, of suffering
The enigmas of the day, every hardy opposition

Of opinion, and every gain of hard-constructed good,
Music of furor, or insights passive and sovereign

When the clearest dreams are in a half-lit wakefulness,
When the best love is untutored, able to be blessed.

It is the style of the mariner proud on his vessel,
Who keeps a weather eye to the storm, but hopes,

Aware of the improbable, weather will not alter
From gentle zephyrs allowing him the spectacle of July

As if the afternoon were perfect and endless,
Porpoises in pairs follow the ship, and seals

Poke up their hopeful heads to see what trespasses.
The lobsterman is still at pulling his traps,

And far off the race jockeys on its summer errands,
Lightly touched with an ethereal evanescence,

Before returning to the home clubhouse and yacht club,
Inevitably pulling down the small sails at nightfall.

So should reality seem to be a style
Consummate and faultless, held in the hand

As the tooled wheel before the magnetic compass,
And all should be orderly in earth as in heaven.

But that we know the gale will rive us,
Years cut down our vanities, time unseam us,

Force throw the weak baby seal to death
On the rocks, the unexpected shock sink the vessel,

Or worse, to see the oncoming rollers and savage tempest
And know our doom forced against any wood or canvas,

Where is the style then for man the master of earth
And of waters, man who thinks to control his life

And to roam through the black new wastes of space
As if he had comfort in his small, cramping capsule?

Is there an outer misadventure or foul catastrophe
So malign as the malevolent sunderings of the soul?

For down in the depths of the heart's adventure
The evil in man since the loss of Paradise

And that knowledge which came in the Garden of Eden
When Eve offered man the fruit of the womb and of life

Has taken every stride with his heavenward hope
And locked his going in his ever knowing dualism,

So that from the opposites of good and evil, flesh and spirit,
Damnation and redemption, he is never absent

But truly is fixed in a vise of these opposites
Contending manly, forcing his sperm on children,

Unable not to start the chain of being again,
Crying out again and again when he sees suffering.

Is it not a provocation of the spirit of unity,
That, despite the ramifications of disparate phenomena,

Man seizes immortality on the instant
And can make his watery flesh seem permanent

In the magical power of a given poem,
In the working of paint, in the modelling of stone,

In the flash and controlled passion of music,
Is not the style of the man caught in his art,

And is art itself not a triumph of nature,
Before the worm takes over, before the breakneck tomb?

I sing the harmony of the instant of knowing
When all things dual become a unity,

The power of the mind to envisage singleness,
The purpose of the hand to shape lovingness.

If I sing Aeschylean right-mindedness,
It is of myself mostly that I sing,

Hoping the improbable advent of unity
Will triumph over the mocking dualisms

Which, each seeming real, yearly tore me
In the macerations of their blooded factions

As, whether to fly out, and shout with the government,
Or, silent as a crab, burrow in the sands of solitude;

Whether to embark upon the waves of chance,
Or reside in some closed nook of contemplation;

Whether to accept the brotherhood of the many,
Or live for the talents and the truths of the few.

So should style amplify and refine man's poise,
Be an instrument as lucid as the best of his knowing.

THE WATER-PIPE

Do you remember, Bharati,
When you brought your water-pipe
From far, sepulchral India
To our evening in white-hot Cambridge?

A Princess among the intellectuals!
And your brown, brown flesh
Flashed under your Eastern sari?
I loved you subtly then, Bharati;

Unattainable Princess of India.
When I smoked your water-pipe,
Returning the stem, you would wipe
It carefully with a silken handkerchief.

But when you smoked my Western pipe
You grasped it and sucked in tobacco
As you would drink the West; nor wiped
The pipe stem, Bharati, Princess of India.

EAGLES

Nature's secrets are ever subtle.
After every human failure
Still she astounds the eye
With natural majesty.

Inherent in the able day
Is a source so pure and keen
It overwhelms the senses
With the newly seen.

The newly seen that is ancient
And touches our deepest heart
Under the chords of remembrance
Where belief would leap and start.

I saw three bald eagles
Flying over Undercliff
In ancient majesty and power.
My heart leaped up stiff

At so tremendous a sight,
Those great, rare birds in search,
Their strange cries gutteral,
One on a dead tree perched,

Then in unison and swift flight,
As if purpose were absolute,
They flew passionate, inexorable,
And wheeled from my sight.

MAY EVENING

Long after our departure
Someone in a moment of significant rapture,
Seeing a boy beside a fountain,
Watched by an elder in a garden,
Will think that the past is the future
And the present is both.

We live in the imagination of the moment
When in a harmonious instant of apprehension
Subtle dreams are reality.
A boy playing by a fountain, unselfconscious,
A man watching him, studious in a garden,
Partake of immortality.

I am my father's father, or farther back,
Some enchanted man of the twelfth century;
I am Socrates' questioner in the agora,
I am a child dancing on the green seen by Blake,
I am all those to whom a moment has meant
A spell of rapture and a gift of grace.

The boy deploys from the playing water,
The man with his visions goes to get some coffee,
The incredible elan of the springtide evening
Lingers but departs; the graceful salute of the static
Moment of happiness and concord is given.
Fate outlasts the flash. Recognition was on us.

THE GESTURE

From the drama of horror and despair,
Out of the window, over the casket,
Young girls are bringing spring flowers
Carried and proffered in a spring basket.

So light a gesture in so grave a time.
I am one who, flailed and threshed,
Wishes in his power to understand
What it is that death refreshed.

An intimate gesture of young girls.
The flowers are laid before her white face.
In the mystery of their understanding
Reposes what we know of grace.

THE FACE, THE AXE, AND TIME

We survive for a while, and then we die.
While we are going we feel pure and free.
Each thinks the axe will fall on someone else.
Each hoping heart leaps in its instancy.
No man has stood still as a tree.
Each face has a unique radiancy.

We feel strong, but something stronger
Eradicates our avid sense of order.
When the flowers appear they are already gone,
Our mind sinks although we linger longer,
Time is a spender, not a hoarder,
Every old deer was once a faun.

THE KILLER

On the Assassination of President Kennedy

There I go, with an inscrutable face,
Controlled by the gunsight of hate.
My own accuser, raging with despair,
I kill the clean American air.

All dreams of love are dim.
I kill myself in killing him.
I am of Satan, the expression
Of evil will through my aggression.

I do not know what I do.
Vileness is deep, is ever new.
My fate is to have been sent
To kill my own friend and President.

I do not know what I do.
Love left me. No love was true.
I did now know I sealed my fate
In denying love to love but hate.

Hate woke hate. My savage fashion
Begot an equally savage passion.
The bullet that shocked a nation
Came back to bring my own annihilation,

Came back in such Satanic style
Justice is denied my trial.
I reduced to savagery
Those who could have made my spirit free.

ACTION AND POETRY

The poet against society: stay away from him.
He sees, but cannot help: passionate disability
Allows him to do nothing about human error.
He broods upon the consequence of action,

Wishing some brave intelligence could conquer pain,
Devise a way amid labyrinthian involvements;
He feels the brutality and affront of suffering,
He clings to a remnant of man's nobility.

It is the brutal and primitive power of the poet
Raises him to his source and height;
From darkness, desolation, his sympathetic projection
Touches the heart when the heart is alight.

Keep far away from the reality of the poet
Unless you, too, have suffered the worst,
And cling down some deep region of belief
To the naked courage in the heart of man.

FISHING FOR SNAKES

Fishing for snakes
In the wide well of summertime
Depends upon the kind of rake
Best nets their slidy shine.

They will slip a butterfly net,
Which is too delicate, unsubtle,
But if persistent you can catch them yet,
On your belly in a downward effort.

It is an extension of the hand
In the rake like a fan, and firm,
Wide, with fingers in a fixed half clench
Will sweep the well and fault their swim.

It is all a kind of trick,
Obscured in method, but never despair.
After exertion, with a certain flick,
You can fling them up in the air.

I don't say that I would kill one,
Although this is nothing to shun,
But I like to see the fellows run,
Wriggling away in an evil sun.

AT MC SORLEY'S BAR

I

In the time of proverbs and vision
I beheld the brutalities of the day
As one who would look the other way.
Such was the power of my derision

That I, hooked in a haven of Paradise,
Said, let the fallen man see
His original immortality
And break out of the human vise,

But he was so enamored of Hell
That he clutched at his blood
And fell in a foul flood
Which he thought was very well,

But when I made up the words and sign,
Able to distinguish and to acclaim
A moral purpose in man's aim,
I proved his fallen life was mine.

II

I saw him fallen in the aisle,
Fallen on the sawdust floor,
His spirit would not soar,
His deepest love was to be vile.

From having seen too much of life
And known that suffering was sure
He had no heart to seek the pure
And everything he saw was blear.

With sympathy and empathy
I could not raise him up again,
Nor stop the beauty of his pain,
For all my lust and energy.

THE ILLUSION OF ETERNITY

Things of this world
In pure afternoons of gold,
And splendor of October,
Radiant air, still trees,
Give the illusion of eternity.

As if there were no suffering,
No ancient heart-ache of the being,
No tortures of the soul,
No struggle with mortality,
But changelessness, eternity.

A leaf falls here and there.
There are small birds a-chirp,
A chipmunk on a pine tree,
No cloud in the sky,
October afternoon, gold rarity.

Through the transparent air
Time is a kind of singing
In the inner being,
Acceptable singing,
Giving the illusion of eternity.

THE RUSH

When the wind is stirring in the evening,
Enchanting the senses, and then it lets down
And the moon comes up making a stillness
Taking away the meanings of man and town,

It is good to be out of the mind entirely,
In another dimension of joy and dance,
And dance in the madness of the senses,
Moon-crazed in meadows, avid of glance

To worlds that the rational heart craves
In a world of the irrational,
Elevated to immediacy
In the rhythms of the passional,

And to be so alive as to feel
In dancing foot the root of the real,
Immortal sky upon your eye
And now a soft wind will sigh

As the moon wanes, you will retreat
From ecstatic vision beyond faith
And in later times beyond belief
Dream of the world of the wraith—

Like purity you knew when dream
And reality were one unity
And the world of the senses
Was everything of immortality you could see.

THE ECHOING ROCKS

Far out to sea on the ocean side
We passed shore-distant islands in mid-haze
At mid-day; then I was startled when I heard
The distant, strange islands, vaguely visible,
Give forth transgressions of striking sounds.
They tumbled, cracked, and laughed, and overwhelmed
Sea's empty distances, coming to me
Like ancient myths rising in the feelings,
Slashing, and running along, inhabiting Greece
Her lucky and fatal shores, long racing down
Portentous centuries, and it seemed as if sirens
Rose and descended in toxic, timeless allurement.
Strange sounds going back to dawn
When man was coming up into his own feeling,
Out of the sea. Sounds like some great wash

Of being. Supreme articulation of nothingness,
Concentration of the strength of purest dreaming.
I dream the siren-sounding shore to poetry,
(Articulate nothingness out of the depths of me)
I stand to visionary, imaginary glory
As we pass the echoing rocks and lose their story.

OFF PEMAQUID

The ocean rolling in its rising wave,
An oncome of a massing danger, our weak lip
Holds helm, and we would let her rave,
Man's peacock with her feathers buoyant,
And we would strut her; all that watery enclave,

Vast ocean upholding our little size
As we fare onward, north and eastward,
Daring a song, although we may capsize.
We keep our compass on magnetic course
Though seas mount up, man always tries.

And so we make to far, expected landfalls
Long suffering the waves of chance,
Rolling and standing to the sea bells' calls
In ancient challenge, and in nimble dance
Small man, great ocean hurled down heavy malls.

THE MATIN PANDEMONIUMS

Begin before birth with swept-back fins.
Among animals and birds there are no echoes,
They live in an exorbitancy of orchestration.
It is the greatness of nature rides up the air
With such rich morning calls; the fleet shepherd

Lives in love of action; the goat has delicate steps;
The swan is the lord of all he surveys.
He surveys golden pheasant, accomplished tortoise.

One sees from the porch of the imagination
Fabulous oncome and arising of the world,
The get of jets, choiring high and rangy.
What is this talk of separation and anguish,
Where is there deeper secret revelation than among
The early morning pandemoniums of the birds?

ORDEAL

Enriched by death a thousandfold,
To that kingdom of nothingness still I come.
The arrogance of the ego, my eager master,
Is put down by savage death and made dumb.

Love, affection, probability, tender hopes, onlook
Even to perfection in the heights of the mind
Are made the laughing stock of the years,
When the master of savagery makes us blind.

Even the old Greeks fail us, with only
Stasis to hold us in life's precarious place.
Two crossed sticks are a deeper myth:
Let him who will look radiance in the face.

TONES OF SPRING

If I could only express
The mauve light of a Spring evening,

If I could only catch the words on the wing,
The spectacular mauve of a Spring evening,

If I could only capture the cries
Of Canadian geese flying north in April,

If only the light, incomparable, would never diminish,
If only the love of the world were ever total,

If ever the love we feel and cherish
Were never destroyed by fate to make us fatal,

If only the incomparable light through the window
Of the soul as through the window in the evening

Could exist immiscible, be immitigable,
And if only the poem were perfect,

As we dream perfection when our love is strongest,
If I could only express mauves of an inexpressible ineluctability,

The deeper tones that are coming through the window,
The darker statures that are standing in the soul,

The radiancy of the language that is elusive,
Angels that protect us from the darkening of the evening,

The deeper tones that are of a strong imperfection,
And darkness now appears upon the panes,

The dark substratum strains to meet the intellect,
The unalterable truth raves about the street,

If I could only express superiority
To devils and angels to be free,

I would penetrate the great, shadowy stage
On which the highest words are thrown, and save.

Index of First Lines

Index of First Lines

New Directions Paperbooks

Prince Ilango Adigal, *Shilappadikaram:
The Ankle Bracelet.* NDP162.
Corrado Alvaro, *Revolt in Aspromonte.*
NDP119.
Chairil Anwar, *Selected Poems.* WPS2.
Djuna Barnes, *Nightwood.* NDP98.
Charles Baudelaire, *Flowers of Evil.*† NDP71.
Eric Bentley, *Bernard Shaw.* NDP59.
Jorge Luis Borges, *Labyrinths.* NDP186.
Alain Bosquet, *Selected Poems.*† WPS4.
Paul Bowles, *The Sheltering Sky.* NDP158.
Kay Boyle, *Thirty Stories.* NDP62.
Breakthrough to Peace. (Anthology) NDP124.
William Bronk, *The World, the Worldless.*
(SFR) NDP157.
Buddha, *The Dhammapada.*
(Babbitt translation) NDP160.
Louis-Ferdinand Céline,
Journey to the End of the Night. NDP84.
Blaise Cendrars, *Selected Writings.*† NDP203.
Bankim-chandra Chatterjee,
Krishnakanta's Will. NDP120.
Michal Choromanski, *Jealousy and Medicine.*
NDP165.
Jean Cocteau, *The Holy Terrors.* NDP212.
Maurice Collis,
The Land of the Great Image. NDP76.
Marco Polo. NDP93.
Contemporary German Poetry.†
(Anthology) NDP148.
Gregory Corso,
Happy Birthday of Death. NDP86.
Long Live Man. NDP127.
David Daiches, *Virginia Woolf.*
(Revised) NDP96.
Richard Eberhart, *Selected Poems.* NDP198.
Russell Edson, *The Very Thing That Happens.*
NDP137.
William Empson,
Seven Types of Ambiguity. NDP204.
Some Versions of Pastoral. NDP92.
Lawrence Ferlinghetti,
A Coney Island of the Mind. NDP74.
Her. NDP88.
Routines. NDP187.
*Starting from San Francisco.** Gift Edition.
NDP169.
Unfair Arguments with Existence. NDP143.
Ronald Firbank, *Two Novels.* NDP128.
Dudley Fitts,
Poems from the Greek Anthology. NDP60.
F. Scott Fitzgerald, *The Crack-up.* NDP54.
Gustave Flaubert, *Sentimental Education.*
NDP63
M. K. Gandhi, *Gandhi on Non-Violence.*
(ed. Thomas Merton) NDP197.
André Gide, *Dostoevsky.* NDP100.

Goethe, *Faust,* Part I.
(MacIntyre translation) NDP70.
Albert J. Guerard, *Thomas Hardy.* NDP185.
James B. Hall, *Us He Devours*
(SFR) NDP156.
Henry Hatfield, *Goethe.* NDP136.
Thomas Mann. (Revised Edition) NDP101.
John Hawkes, *The Cannibal.* NDP123.
The Lime Twig. NDP95.
Second Skin. NDP146.
Hermann Hesse, *Siddhartha.* NDP65.
Edwin Honig, *García Lorca.*
(Revised) NDP102.
Ann Hutchinson, *Labanotation.* NDP104.
Christopher Isherwood, *The Berlin Stories.*
NDP134.
Henry James, *Stories of Writers and Artists.*
NDP57.
Alfred Jarry, *Ubu Roi.* NDP105.
James Joyce, *Stephen Hero.* NDP133.
Franz Kafka, *Amerika.* NDP117.
Bob Kaufman,
Solitudes Crowded with Loneliness. NDP199.
Hugh Kenner, *Wyndham Lewis.* NDP167.
Lincoln Kirstein,
Rhymes & More Rhymes of a Pfc. NDP202.
de Laclos, *Dangerous Acquaintances.* NDP61.
P. Lal, translator, *Great Sanskrit Plays.*
NDP142.
Tommaso Landolfi,
Gogol's Wife and Other Stories. NDP155.
Lautréamont, *Maldoror.* NDP207.
Denise Levertov, *O Taste and See.* NDP149.
The Jacob's Ladder. NDP112.
Harry Levin, *James Joyce.* NDP87.
García Lorca, *Selected Poems.*† NDP114.
Three Tragedies. NDP52.
Carson McCullers, *The Member of the
Wedding.* (Playscript) NDP153.
Thomas Merton,
Bread in the Wilderness. NDP91.
Clement of Alexandria. Gift Edition.
NDP173.
Emblems of a Season of Fury. NDP140.
*Original Child Bomb.** Gift Edition.
NDP174.
Raids on the Unspeakable. NDP213.
Selected Poems. NDP85.
Henry Miller,
Big Sur & Oranges of Hieronymus Bosch.
NDP161.
The Colossus of Maroussi. NDP75.
The Cosmological Eye. NDP109.
Henry Miller on Writing. NDP151.
Remember to Remember. NDP111.
*The Smile at the Foot of the Ladder.**
Gift Edition. NDP176.

Henry Miller,
  Sunday After the War. NDP110.
  The Time of the Assassins. NDP115.
  The Wisdom of the Heart. NDP94.
Yukio Mishima, *Death in Midsummer.*
  NDP215.
Eugenio Montale, *Selected Poems.*† NDP193.
Vladimir Nabokov, *Nikolai Gogol.* NDP78.
New Directions 17. (Anthology) NDP103.
New Directions 18. (Anthology) NDP163.
New Directions 19. (Anthology) NDP214.
George Oppen,
  The Materials. (SFR) NDP122.
  This In Which. (SFR) NDP201.
Wilfred Owen, *Collected Poems.* NDP210.
Boris Pasternak, *Safe Conduct.* NDP77.
Kenneth Patchen, *Because It Is.* NDP83.
  Doubleheader. NDP211.
  The Journal of Albion Moonlight. NDP99.
  Memoirs of a Shy Pornographer. NDP205.
  Selected Poems. NDP160.
  Plays for a New Theater. (Anthology)
    NDP216.
Ezra Pound, *ABC of Reading.* NDP89.
  Classic Noh Theatre of Japan. NDP79,
  The Confucian Odes. NDP81.
  Confucius to Cummings. (Anthology)
    NDP126.
  Love Poems of Ancient Egypt. Gift Edition.
    NDP178.
  Selected Poems. NDP66.
  Translations.† (Enlarged Edition) NDP145.
Philip Rahv, *Image and Idea.* NDP67.
Herbert Read, *The Green Child.* NDP208.
Jesse Reichek, *Etcetera.* NDP196.
Kenneth Rexroth, *Assays.* NDP113.
  Bird in the Bush. NDP80.
  The Homestead Called Damascus. WPS3.
  Natural Numbers. (Selected Poems)
    NDP141.
  100 Poems from the Chinese. NDP192.
  100 Poems from the Japanese.† NDP147.
Charles Reznikoff,
  By the Waters of Manhattan. (SFR)
    NDP121.

Charles Reznikoff,
  Testimony: The United States 1885–1890.
    (SFR) NDP200.
Arthur Rimbaud, *Illuminations.*† NDP56.
  Season in Hell & Drunken Boat.† NDP97.
San Francisco Review Annual No. 1.
  (SFR) NDP138.
Jean-Paul Sartre, *Nausea.* NDP82.
Stevie Smith, *Selected Poems.* NDP159.
Stendhal, *Lucien Leuwen.*
  Book I: *The Green Huntsman.* NDP107.
  Book II: *The Telegraph.* NDP108.
Jules Supervielle, *Selected Writings.*† NDP209.
Dylan Thomas, *Adventures in the Skin Trade.*
  NDP183.
  A Child's Christmas in Wales. Gift Edition.
    NDP181.
  Portrait of the Artist as a Young Dog.
    NDP51.
  Quite Early One Morning. NDP90.
  Under Milk Wood. NDP73.
Norman Thomas, *Ask at the Unicorn.*
  NDP129.
Lionel Trilling, *E. M. Forster.* NDP189.
Paul Valéry, *Selected Writings.*† NDP184.
Nathanael West, *Miss Lonelyhearts &*
  Day of the Locust. NDP125.
George F. Whicher, tr.,
  The Goliard Poets.† NDP206.
Tennessee Williams,
  The Glass Menagerie. NDP218.
  In the Winter of Cities. NDP154.
  27 Wagons Full of Cotton. NDP217.
William Carlos Williams,
  In the American Grain. NDP53.
  The Farmers' Daughters. NDP106.
  Many Loves. NDP191.
  Paterson. Complete. NDP152.
  Pictures from Brueghel.
    (Pulitzer Prize) NDP118.
  Selected Poems. NDP131.
Curtis Zahn,
  American Contemporary. (SFR) NDP139.

* Paperbound over boards.　　† Bilingual.
(SFR) A New Directions / San Francisco Review Book.

Complete descriptive catalog available free on request from
New Directions, 333 Sixth Avenue, New York 10014.